MEDIA OWNERSHIP

MEDIA OWNERSHIP

HAROLD F. VELLIOTIS
EDITOR

Nova Science Publishers, Inc.
New York

For permission to use material from this book please contact us:
Telephone 631-231-7269; Fax 631-231-8175
Web Site: http://www.novapublishers.com

LIBRARY OF CONGRESS CATALOGING-IN-PUBLICATION DATA
Media ownership / Editor, Harold F. Velliotis.
ix, 117 p. ; 23 cm.
Includes bibliographical references and index.
ISBN 978-1-60692-365-8 (softcover)
1. Mass media --Ownership --United States. 2. Telecommunication --Ownership --United States. I. Velliotis, Harold F.
P96.E252 U663 2009
302.230973

2009288358

Published by Nova Science Publishers, Inc. † New York

CONTENTS

PREFACE

The media industry plays an important role in educating and entertaining the public. While the media industry provides the public with many national choices, media outlets located in a local market are more likely to provide local programs that meet the needs of residents in the market compared to national outlets. This book reviews (1) the number and ownership of various media outlets; (2) the level of minority- and women-owned broadcast outlets; (3) the influence of economic, legal and regulatory, and technological factors on the number and ownership of media outlets; and (4) stakeholders' opinions on modifying certain media ownership laws and regulations.

Chaper 1 - The media industry plays an important role in educating and entertaining the public. While the media industry provides the public with many national choices, media outlets located in a local market are more likely to provide local programs that meet the needs of residents in the market compared to national outlets. This report reviews (1) the number and ownership of various media outlets; (2) the level of minority- and women-owned broadcast outlets; (3) the influence of economic, legal and regulatory, and technological factors on the number and ownership of media outlets; and (4) stakeholders' opinions on modifying certain media ownership laws and regulations.

Chapter 2 - The Federal Communications Commission's (FCC or Commission) broadcast media ownership rules are intended to foster the three long-standing goals of U.S. media policy — competition, localism, and diversity of voices. The FCC has the statutory obligation to review these rules every four years to determine if they continue to serve the public interest or should be modified or eliminated. In December 2007, the FCC adopted an order that modified only one of its broadcast media ownership rules — the newspaper-broadcast cross-ownership rule — and left the other rules intact.

Under the new rule, it would be presumptively "not inconsistent with" the public interest, in the 20 largest local markets, for an entity to own both a major daily newspaper and a single television or radio station, so long as the television station is not among the four highest-rated stations in the market and after the transaction there are at least eight independently owned and operating major media voices. Otherwise, in most situations newspaper-broadcast cross-ownership in a local market would be presumptively inconsistent with the public interest. Each proposed combination, however, would be reviewed on a case-by-case basis, and proposed combinations in smaller markets could be approved. Fifteen parties have appealed the new rule; the challenges will be heard by the United States Court of Appeals for the Ninth Circuit. A joint resolution of disapproval (S.J.Res. 28) to revoke the new rule was approved on a voice vote of the Senate on May 15, 2008, and a similar resolution has been introduced in the House (H.J.Res. 79). In addition, S. 2332 and H.R. 4835 would negate the rule because they would require the FCC, before adopting any new broadcast ownership rule after October 1, 2007, to give 90 days' notice for public comment, which was not done prior to adoption of the rule. In contrast, H.R. 4167 would eliminate the newspaper-radio (but not newspaper-television) cross-ownership prohibition in its entirety.

In its previous quadrennial review, in June 2003, the FCC modified five of its broadcast media ownership rules, easing restrictions on the ownership of multiple television stations (nationally and in local markets) and on local media cross-ownership, and tightening restrictions on the ownership of multiple radio stations in local markets. Those rules have never gone into effect. Sec. 629 of the FY2004 Consolidated Appropriations Act (P.L. 108-199) instructed the FCC to modify its new National Television Ownership rule to allow a broadcast network to own and operate local broadcast stations that reach, in total, at most 39% of U.S. television households. In June 2004, the United States Court of Appeal for the Third Circuit, in *Prometheus Radio Project vs. Federal Communications Commission,* found that the FCC did not provide reasoned analysis to support its specific local ownership limits, and also that the FCC failed to address the impact of it new rules on minority ownership of broadcast stations, and therefore remanded portions of the new local ownership rules back to the FCC and extended its stay of those rules.

Chapter 3 - The media play an important role in educating and entertaining the public and fostering an informed citizenry; thus the ownership of media outlets has been a long-standing concern of the Congress. The Federal Communications Commission (FCC) regulates many aspects of the media industry, including radio and television stations and cable and satellite service. In the Telecommunications Act of 1996 (1996 Act), the Congress required that FCC periodically review its media ownership rules. In 2003, FCC released an order that altered its existing media ownership rules. This order generated significant public debate, and more than 500,000 comments were filed with FCC. The U.S. Court of Appeals for the Third Circuit affirmed some of FCC's rule changes while remanding others for further justification or modification; [1] most of the rule changes have not gone into effect. In response to the court's decision and the congressional mandate for periodic review of its rules, FCC has another proceeding underway to assess its media ownership rules. This proceeding has attracted significant attention from both the public and the Congress, and has raised concerns about the level of consolidation in the media industry.

In: Media Ownership
Editor: Harold F. Velliotis, pp. 1-65
ISBN 978-1-60692-365-8

Chapter 1

MEDIA OWNERSHIP: ECONOMIC FACTORS INFLUENCE THE NUMBER OF MEDIA OUTLETS IN LOCAL MARKETS, WHILE OWNERSHIP BY MINORITIES AND WOMEN APPEARS LIMITED AND IS DIFFICULT TO ASSESS*

United States Government Accountability Office

WHY GAO DID THIS STUDY

The media industry plays an important role in educating and entertaining the public. While the media industry provides the public with many national choices, media outlets located in a local market are more likely to provide local programs that meet the needs of residents in the market compared to national outlets. This report reviews (1) the number and ownership of various media outlets; (2) the level of minority- and women-owned broadcast outlets; (3) the influence of economic, legal and regulatory, and technological factors on the number and ownership of media outlets; and (4) stakeholders' opinions on modifying certain media ownership laws and regulations.

* Excerpted from GAO Report 08-383, dated March 2008.

GAO conducted case studies of 16 randomly sampled markets, stratified by population. GAO also interviewed officials from the Federal Communications Commission (FCC), the Department of Commerce, trade associations, and the industry. Finally, GAO reviewed FCC's forms, processes, and reports.

What GAO Found

The numbers of media outlets and owners of media outlets generally increase with the size of the market; markets with large populations have more television and radio stations and newspapers than less populated markets. Additionally, diverse markets have more outlets operating in languages other than English, contributing to a greater number of outlets. Some companies participate in operating agreements wherein two or more media outlets might, for example, share content. As such, these agreements may suggest that the number of independently owned media outlets might not always be a good indicator of how many independently produced local news and other programs are available in a market. Finally, the Internet is expanding access to media content and competition.

On a biennial basis, FCC collects data on the gender, race, and ethnicity of broadcast owners to, according to FCC, position itself and the Congress to assess the need for, and success of, programs to foster minority and women ownership. However, these data suffer from three weaknesses: (1) exemptions from filing for certain types of broadcast stations, (2) inadequate data quality procedures, and (3) problems with data storage and retrieval. These weaknesses limit the benefits of this data collection effort. While reliable government data are lacking, available evidence suggests that ownership of broadcast outlets by minorities and women is limited. Several barriers contribute to the limited levels of ownership by these groups, including a lack of easy access to sufficient capital.

A variety of economic, legal and regulatory, and technological factors influence media ownership. Two economic factors—high fixed costs and the size of the market—appear to influence the number of media outlets in a market, the incentive to consolidate, and the prevalence of operating agreements. By limiting the number and types of media outlets that a company can own, various laws and regulations affect the ownership of media outlets. Technological factors, such as the emergence of the Internet, have facilitated entry for new companies, thereby increasing the amount of content and competition.

Stakeholders expressed varied opinions on modifications to media ownership rules. Most business stakeholders expressing an opinion on various media ownership rules were more likely to report that the rules should be relaxed or repealed. In contrast, nonbusiness stakeholders who expressed an opinion on the rules were more likely to report that the rules should be left in place or strengthened. Both business and nonbusiness stakeholders who expressed an opinion on a previously repealed tax certificate program supported either reinstating or expanding the program to encourage the sale of broadcast outlets to minorities.

ABBREVIATIONS

DBS	direct broadcast satellite
DMA	Designated Market Area
FCC	Federal Communications Commission
MSA	metropolitan statistical area
MVPD	multichannel video program distributor
NTIA	National Telecommunications and Information Administration
PBS	Public Broadcasting Service
UHF	ultra-high frequency

March 12, 2008
The Honorable Edward J. Markey
Chairman
Subcommittee on Telecommunications and the Internet Committee on
Energy and Commerce,
House of Representatives

Dear Mr. Chairman:

The media play an important role in educating and entertaining the public and fostering an informed citizenry. Since the nation's founding, newspapers have gathered and disseminated the news of the day, thereby helping citizens become informed voters. In the early 20th century, the emergence of radio and television expanded the options for educating and entertaining the public, and in the 21st century, the Internet delivers information and entertainment from a virtually limitless supply of sources. Whereas most citizens were formerly limited to a newspaper or newspapers in their local area, citizens today with an Internet connection can read publications from around the world.

Given the vital role of the media in American life, the ownership of media outlets has been a long-standing concern of the Congress. The Federal Communications Commission (FCC) regulates many aspects of the media industry, including radio and television stations and cable and satellite service. In the Telecommunications Act of 1996 (1996 Act), the Congress required that FCC periodically review its broadcast ownership rules [1]. In 2003, FCC released an order that altered its existing broadcast ownership rules. This order generated significant public debate, and more than 500,000 comments were filed with FCC. The U.S. Court of Appeals for the Third Circuit affirmed some of FCC's rule changes while remanding others for further justification or modification [2]. In response to the court's decision and the congressional mandate for periodic review of its rules FCC opened another proceeding to assess its broadcast ownership rules. This proceeding also attracted significant attention from both the public and the Congress, with concerns arising about the level of consolidation in the media industry. On February 4, 2008, FCC released a rule concluding its latest review of the broadcast ownership rules.

While today's media environment provides the public with numerous programming choices from across the country, media outlets in local markets remain a concern for policymakers. With cable and satellite service, the public can receive programming from nationwide outlets, such as CNN and FOX News, and television stations in adjacent markets. However, media outlets located in a market are more likely to provide local news, public affairs, and political programming addressing the needs of residents in that market, such as coverage of local political campaigns, compared to nationwide and adjacent-market outlets. Reflecting the importance of local media outlets, localism is one of FCC's three policy goals for media ownership, along with competition and diversity.

You asked us to examine the current status of media ownership. On December 14, 2007, we provided preliminary information on our review of media ownership [3] This report discusses (1) the number and ownership of various media outlets; (2) the level of minority- and women-owned broadcast outlets; (3) the influence of economic, legal and regulatory, and technological factors on the number and ownership of media outlets; and (4) stakeholders' opinions on modifying certain media ownership laws and regulations.

To respond to the objectives of this report, we interviewed officials from FCC, the National Telecommunications and Information Administration (NTIA) of the Department of Commerce, and trade associations. Additionally, we interviewed 102 industry officials and experts, selected based on industry sector (radio and television stations, broadcast networks, newspapers, cable, satellite, and Internet), geographic service territory, size of the media outlet, and professional publications (for experts). See appendix III for a complete list of individuals and organizations that we interviewed. To assess the number and ownership of media outlets, we conducted case studies in 16 Nielsen Designated Market Areas (DMA) [4]. To select the 16 case study markets, we used a stratified random sample methodology: we (1) randomly selected 4 case study markets from each of 3 market strata (large, medium, and small), [5] (2) selected the 3 largest markets as a separate stratum, [6] and (3) judgmentally selected 1 market from the medium-size category to test our data collection and structured interview methodology [7]. The 16 markets that we analyzed include approximately 20 percent of all television households in the United States. In each case study market, we identified the number of television and radio stations, newspapers (daily and weekly), and cable and satellite television operators present in the central city of the DMA. We also identified the number of owners of these outlets. We did not identify low-power stations or local Web pages. See appendix I for a more detailed discussion of our overall scope and methodology.

We conducted this performance audit from February 2007 through March 2008 in accordance with generally accepted government auditing standards. Those standards require that we plan and perform the audit to obtain sufficient, appropriate evidence to provide a reasonable basis for our findings and conclusions based on our audit objectives. We believe that the evidence obtained provides a reasonable basis for our findings and conclusions based on our audit objectives.

Results in Brief

The numbers of media outlets and owners of media outlets generally increase with the size of the market, although operating agreements may reduce the effective number of independent outlets. Markets with large populations have more radio and television stations and newspapers than less populated markets. For example, in New York City, the nation's largest market, we identified 21 television stations and 73 radio stations. In contrast, we found 2 television stations and 16 radio stations in Harrisonburg, Virginia, the smallest market in our review. In more diverse markets, we also observed more radio and television stations and newspapers operating in languages other than English, which contributed to a greater number of outlets. Some companies participate in agreements to share content or agreements that allow one entity to produce programming or sell advertising through two outlets, among other agreements. In our review, these agreements were prevalent in a variety of markets but not in the top three markets, suggesting that market size may influence the benefits that firms achieve through such arrangements. To some degree, these agreements may suggest that the number of independently owned media outlets in a market might not always be a good indicator of how many independently produced local news or other programs are available in a market [8]. For example, in Wilkes Barre/Scranton, Pennsylvania, we identified eight television stations and seven owners; however, because of various operating agreements, there are three loose commercial groupings in the market. While the numbers of outlets and owners vary with market size, the Internet is expanding access to media content and competition. For example, individuals can access content from a virtually limitless supply of sources. However, we observed few independent news Web sites in our case study markets, as most of the Web sites that we found were affiliated with one or more traditional media outlets.

Ownership of broadcast outlets by minorities and women appears limited, but comprehensive data are lacking. FCC collects data on the gender, race, and ethnicity of radio and television station owners biennially through its Ownership Report for Commercial Broadcast Stations, or Form 323. However, we found that these data suffer from three weaknesses: (1) exemptions from filing for certain types of broadcast stations, such as noncommercial stations; (2) inadequate data quality procedures; and (3) problems with data storage and retrieval. While reliable government data on ownership by minorities and women are lacking, available evidence from industry stakeholders and experts we interviewed, as well as government and nongovernment reports, suggest that ownership of broadcast outlets by these groups is limited. For example, reports by Free Press, a nongovernmental organization, found that women and minorities own about 5 percent and 3 percent of full-power television stations, respectively, and about 6 percent and 8 percent of full-power radio stations, respectively [9]. We identified three primary barriers contributing to the limited levels of ownership by minorities and women. These barriers include (1) the large scale of ownership in the media industry, (2) a lack of easy access to sufficient capital for financing the purchases of stations, and (3) the repeal of the tax certificate program—which allowed for the deferral of capital gains taxes on the sale of broadcast outlets and thereby provided financial incentives for incumbents to sell stations to minorities. Because more accurate, complete, and reliable data would allow FCC to better assess the impact of its rules and regulations and allow the Congress to make more informed legislative decisions, we are recommending that FCC take steps to improve the reliability and accessibility of its data on the gender, race, and ethnicity of broadcast outlet owners.

A variety of economic, legal and regulatory, and technological factors influence media ownership. Two significant economic factors—the prevalence of high fixed costs and the size of the local market—appear to influence the number and ownership of media outlets. For example, high fixed costs produce incentives for companies to consolidate—to own multiple outlets—or develop operating agreements with other companies to distribute content across multiple outlets, thereby spreading the fixed costs across a greater number of outlets. Stakeholders with whom we spoke also cited a variety of legal and regulatory factors that influence the ownership of media outlets. These factors include the local television and radio station ownership limits, FCC's cross-media ownership prohibitions, and the 1996 Act. By limiting the number and types of outlets that a company can own, the laws and regulations affect ownership of media outlets. However, stakeholders held differing views on the level of influence individual policies may have on current ownership. Lastly, stakeholders reported that technological factors, such as the emergence of the Internet, have facilitated entry for new companies, thereby increasing the amount of content and competition. However, stakeholder opinions varied over the significance of new media entrants, such as individual Web pages and blogs.

Stakeholders expressed varied opinions on modifications to media ownership rules, but business stakeholders were more likely to favor deregulation. Most business stakeholders expressing opinions on various media ownership rules were more likely to report that they should be relaxed or repealed. In contrast, nonbusiness stakeholders who expressed opinions on the rules were more likely to report that the rules should be left in place or strengthened. For example, 22 of 31 business stakeholders favored repealing regulations that limit the number of local television and radio stations that a single company can own, while 14 of 19 nonbusiness stakeholders favored strengthening or leaving the rules in place. Similarly, 11 of 22 business stakeholders favored increasing or repealing the cap that limits ownership of television stations nationwide, while 11 of 15 nonbusiness stakeholders favored leaving the cap at its current level or lowering the cap, further restricting ownership of television stations. Alternatively, both business and nonbusiness stakeholders who expressed an opinion on a previously repealed tax certificate program supported either reinstating or expanding the program to encourage the sale of broadcast outlets to minorities.

We provided a draft of this report to FCC for its review and comment. FCC provided technical comments that we incorporated where appropriate. FCC's written comments appear in appendix IV.

Background

FCC regulates many aspects of television and radio station ownership. Laws and regulations limit the ownership of television stations, both nationwide and locally, and limit the ownership of radio stations locally. Since the 1970s, the number of media outlets has increased dramatically, with large increases in the number of television and radio stations; additionally, the number of broadcast networks has increased. More recently however, some segments of the media industry have undergone consolidation, with a few companies acquiring a significant number of outlets.

Laws and Regulations

Through provisions in the Communications Act of 1934, as amended, FCC regulates various aspects of television, radio, cable, and satellite service. FCC has three policy goals for media ownership: competition, diversity, and localism; in the case of diversity, FCC identified viewpoint, outlet, program, source, and minority and female diversity. On December 18, 2007, FCC took action on a number of items impacting media ownership. FCC revised its ban on the ownership of a newspaper and broadcast station in the same market [10]. FCC set a cap on the number of subscribers that a cable operator can serve nationwide and sought comments on vertical ownership limits and cable and broadcast attribution rules [11]. FCC also adopted rules to help new entrants and small businesses, including minority- and women-owned businesses with access to financing, such as modifying the commission's construction permit deadlines, and adopted a notice of proposed rule making that, among other things, sought comment on how best to improve collection of data regarding the gender, race, and ethnicity of broadcast licenses [12]. Finally, FCC adopted a report on broadcast localism and a notice of proposed rule making [13].

Six restrictions on the ownership of television stations, radio stations, and broadcast networks follow:

- *National television ownership cap.* A single entity can own any number of television stations nationwide as long as the stations collectively reach no more than 39 percent of national television households [14]. For purposes of calculating the 39 percent limit, ultra-high frequency (UHF) television stations are attributed with 50 percent of the television households in their market, which FCC refers to as the UHF discount.

- *Local television ownership limit.* A single entity can own two television stations in the same DMA if (1) the "Grade B" contours [15] of the stations do not overlap or (2) at least one of the stations is not ranked among the top four stations in terms of audience share and at least eight independently owned and operating full-power commercial or noncommercial television stations would remain in the DMA.
- *Local radio ownership limit.* A single entity can own up to 5 commercial radio stations, not more than 3 of which are in the same service (that is, AM or FM), in a market with 14 or fewer radio stations, except that an entity can not own, operate, or control more than 50 percent of the stations in a market; up to 6 commercial radio stations, not more than 4 of which are in the same service, in a market with 15 to 29 radio stations; up to 7 commercial radio stations, not more than 4 of which are in the same service, in a market with 30 to 44 radio stations; and up to 8 commercial radio stations, not more than 5 of which are in the same service, in a market with 45 or more radio stations [16].
- *Newspaper-broadcast cross-ownership ban.* Following the effective date of a new approach released by FCC on February 4, 2008, the commission will presume that a proposed newspaper-broadcast transaction is in the public interest if it meets the following test: (1) the market at issue is one of the 20 largest DMAs; (2) the transaction involves the combination of only 1 major daily newspaper and only 1 television or radio station; (3) if the transaction involves a television station, at least 8 independently owned and operating major media voices would remain in the DMA following the transaction; [17] and (4) if the transaction involves a television station, that station s not among the top 4 ranked stations in the DMA. All other proposed newspaper-broadcast transactions would be presumed not in the public interest.18 This new approach will replace an absolute ban, which prohibits a single entity from having common ownership of a full-power television or radio station and a daily newspaper if the television station's "Grade A" contour [19] or the radio station's principal community service area completely encompasses the newspaper's city of publication [20].
- *Television-radio cross-ownership limit.* A single entity can own up to 2 television stations (if permitted under the local television multiple ownership cap) and up to 6 radio stations (if permitted under the local radio multiple ownership cap) or 1 television station and 7 radio stations in a market with at least 20 independently owned media voices remaining post merger; up to 2 television stations and up to 4 radio stations in a

market with at least 10 independently owned media voices remaining post merger; and 1 television station and 1 radio station regardless of the number of independently owned media voices [21].

- *Dual network rule.* A single entity can own multiple broadcast networks, but cannot own two or more of the top four networks (that is, ABC, CBS, FOX, and NBC).

In its December 18, 2007, action, FCC adopted rules limiting the number of subscribers that a cable operator can serve nationwide. While FCC first set limits on the number of subscribers that a cable operator could serve in 1993 and later modified its rules in 1999, the Court of Appeals for the District of Columbia Circuit reversed and remanded those rules [22]. FCC's new rules set the number of subscribers that a cable operator can serve at 30 percent nationwide.

Trends in Media Outlets

Since the 1970s, the number of media outlets has increased dramatically, with large increases in the number of television and radio stations. In the case of television, the number of full-power television stations increased from 875 in 1970 to 1,754 in 2006; this increase occurred in both commercial and noncommercial educational television stations [23]. Moreover, the number of broadcast networks that supply programming to stations across the country increased from three major networks (ABC, CBS, and NBC) to four major networks (ABC, CBS, FOX, and NBC) and several smaller networks, such as The CW Television Network, MY Network TV, and ION Television Network. In the case of radio, the number of full-power radio stations more than doubled, from 6,751 stations in 1970 to 13,793 stations in 2006, with increases in AM, FM, and FM educational stations [24]. Daily newspapers illustrate a different trend—decreasing from 1,763 in 1970 to 1,447 in 2006. While the number of morning newspapers increased from 334 in 1970 to 833 in 2006, the number of evening newspapers decreased by more than half, from 1,429 to 614. Table 1 illustrates the trends in television and radio stations and newspapers Since the 1970s, the number of households subscribing to a multichannel video program distributor (MVPD) has increased significantly, thereby increasing the programming options available to many households. The two most prominent MVPD platforms are cable and direct broadcast satellite (DBS) services. Since 1975, the number of households subscribing to cable service has increased from approximately 10 million to nearly 66 million in 2006, and since 1995, the number of households subscribing to DBS service has increased from 2.2 million to over 29 million in 2006 [25]. Table 2 illustrates the number of cable and DBS subscribers. According to FCC's most recent report on cable industry prices, the average cable operator provided over 70 channels of programming, thereby expanding the programming options available to subscribers of these services [26]. These nonbroadcast networks include a variety of national outlets—such as CNN, Discovery Channel, ESPN, and FOX News—as well as regional outlets—such as the California Channel, Comcast SportsNet Chicago, and New England Cable News.

Table 1. Number of Full-Power Television and Radio Stations and Daily Newspapers

	Number of outlets by year		
Media category	1970	1990	2006
Television stations	875	1,465	1,754
Commercial	691	1,112	1,373
Noncommercial educational	184	353	381
Radio stations	6,751	10,770	13,793
AM	4,269	4,978	4,751
FM	2,083	4,357	6,252
FM educational	399	1,435	2,790
Daily newspapers	1,763	1,643	1,447
Morning	334	559	833
Evening	1,429	1,084	614

Source: GAO analysis of data from FCC and the Newspaper Association of America.

Table 2. Number of Cable and DBS Subscribers

	Subscribers by year (in millions)			
Service	1975	1985	1995	2006
Cable	9.8	35.4	61.6	65.6
DBS	0.0	0.0	2.2	29.1
Total	9.8	35.4	63.8	94.7

Source: GAO analysis of data from FCC; the National Cable and Telecommunications Association; The DirecTV Group, Inc. 1 0-K; and EchoStar Communications Corporation 10-K.

Trends in Media Ownership

While the number of media outlets has increased, the ownership of outlets has evolved. In 1995, FCC eliminated the Financial Interest and Syndication Rules, which had limited the ability of broadcast networks to have ownership interest in programming broadcast on their network [27]. Subsequently, the broadcast networks increasingly became affiliated with companies providing program production services. The Walt Disney Company acquired ABC, Viacom acquired CBS, and NBC joined forces with Universal Pictures. News Corporation—which launched the Fox Broadcasting Network in 1986—also owns several production studios, including 20th Century Fox. Each of the four major broadcast networks owns television stations that reach more than 20 percent of the nation's television households. Other significant owners of television stations include ION Media Networks, Tribune Company, and Broadcasting Media Partners, Inc. [28]. Following passage of the 1996 Act, several companies acquired a large number of radio stations. Clear Channel owned over 1,000 radio stations throughout the United States, and Cumulus Broadcasting and Citadel Communications each owned over 200 stations.

The cable industry also experienced evolution in the ownership of some properties. Cable operators, who distribute programming to subscribers, are pursuing a strategy of regional clustering; this strategy involves acquiring the cable systems throughout a geographic region. In its most recent report on video competition, FCC estimated that there were 118 clusters with approximately 51.5 million subscribers [29]. Comcast and Time Warner Cable have emerged as the largest cable operators, with 26.8 and 16.6 million subscribers, respectively [30]. While cable operators provide many nonbroadcast networks to their subscribers, many nonbroadcast networks are owned by cable operators or broadcast networks. For example, among the nonbroadcast networks with the most subscribers, CNN and TNT are affiliated with Time Warner, ESPN is affiliated with Disney, USA Network is affiliated with NBC-Universal, and Discovery Channel is affiliated with Cox, a large cable operator. On December 18, 2007, FCC adopted a further notice that seeks comment on vertical ownership limits and cable and broadcast attribution rules, including for example, the extent to which vertical integration can lead to foreclosure of entry by unaffiliated programmers.

In recent years, some companies have taken steps to sell assets. In 2005, Viacom split into two separate companies: Viacom and CBS Corporation [31]. The new Viacom includes many of the cable networks, such as MTV and Nickelodeon, and CBS Corporation includes the broadcast network and CBS television and radio stations. In 2006, The McClatchy Company acquired Knight

Ridder, one of the nation's largest newspaper companies, and subsequently sold 12 former Knight Ridder newspapers. For example, The Philadelphia Inquirer and Philadelphia Daily News, former Knight Ridder newspapers, are currently owned by Philadelphia Media Holdings LLC, a private company. Also in 2006, Clear Channel announced plans to sell 448 radio stations, all in markets outside the top 100, and its entire television station group [32]. More recently, The New York Times Company sold its television stations and one of its radio stations. Alternatively, the two satellite radio companies—Sirius and XM—have proposed a merger that, if approved, would leave one company providing satellite radio service.

Numbers of Media Outlets and Owners Generally Increase with Market Size, Although Operating Agreements May Reduce the Effective Number of Independent Outlets

Markets with large populations have more television, radio, and newspaper outlets than less populated markets. In more diverse markets, we also observed more radio and television stations and newspapers operating in languages other than English, which contributed to a greater number of outlets. Some companies participate in agreements to share content or agreements that allow one entity to produce programming or sell advertising through two outlets, among other arrangements.

In our case study markets, these agreements were prevalent in a variety of markets, but not in the top three markets—New York, Los Angeles, and Chicago. Finally, we found that the Internet expands access to media content; however, we observed few news Web sites in our case study markets that were unaffiliated with traditional media outlets.

The Size of Markets Broadly Influences the Number of Media Outlets and Owners

Markets with large populations have more television, radio, and newspaper outlets than less populated media markets.

Additionally, the presence of a large Hispanic population in the media market increases the number of outlets, as owners seek to provide Spanish-language outlets in addition to the full range of English-language outlets supported by the population level.

Top Three Markets

The top three media markets—New York, New York (1); Los Angeles, California (2); and Chicago, Illinois (3)—have several attributes that set them apart from other markets. First, these markets have very large populations. Each of these markets has more than 3 million households. Second, these markets have very diverse populations [33]. For example, New York is the largest African-American media market and the second-largest Asian and Hispanic media market, Los Angeles is the largest Asian and Hispanic media market and the sixth-largest African-American media market, and Chicago is the third-largest African-American media market and the fifth-largest Asian and Hispanic media market. Third, these markets generally have high average household disposable income; [34] the New York market ranks fourth highest in the United States, the Los Angeles market ranks twenty-fourth, and the Chicago market ranks seventh. Finally, these markets also are the production and distribution points for much of the media content in the United States—from films, television shows, and radio programs to magazines and periodicals.The top three media markets differ qualitatively from other markets in the large and varied number of media outlets present in these markets. The combination of large populations and relatively high disposable income helps produce substantial advertising revenues for the media outlets in these markets. These markets have more television and radio stations and more newspapers than other media markets, and competition for cable service from overbuilders also is more likely in these markets [35]. Since these markets have diverse populations, each market has numerous broadcast outlets that provide content in languages other than English. While Spanish is the most common language for non-English media, outlets for content in Chinese, Korean, and other languages are also present [36]. Table 3 indicates how many outlets are located in the top three markets.

FCC's rules allow greater group ownership of media outlets in these three markets because of their size. There are four television duopolies— common ownership of two television stations—in New York, three duopolies in Los Angeles, and three duopolies in Chicago. In addition, several companies own multiple radio stations in these markets; FCC's rules allow for common ownership of eight radio stations, no more than five of which can be in the same service (AM or FM) in these markets. There are some jointly owned newspaper and television stations and newspaper and radio stations in each of these markets [37]. Even with the allowance for group ownership, these three markets still possess a great number of owners who each operate a single broadcast outlet in either radio or television in the respective market. Appendix II provides a more detailed description of the media ownership for all 16 case study markets.

Table 3. Number of Outlets in the Top Three Markets—New York, Los Angeles, and Chicago

	Number of outlets		
Industry segment	New York	Los Angeles	Chicago
Television stations	21	24	16
Radio stations	73	69	65
Daily newspapers	5	2	3

Source: GAO analysis of FCC data, Warren Online Cable and Television Factbook, and *Bowker's News Media Directory*.

Large Markets

Of the four large markets we studied—Miami/Fort Lauderdale, Florida (16); Charlotte, North Carolina (26); Nashville, Tennessee (30); and Wilkes Barre/Scranton, Pennsylvania (53)—the Miami/Fort Lauderdale market has the most television stations and in this respect more closely resembles the top three media markets than the other large media markets [38]. This is due to the large number of Spanish-language outlets present; the Miami/Fort Lauderdale area is the third-largest Hispanic media market in the United States. In addition to television stations, the Miami/Fort Lauderdale market has three daily newspapers, two of which are in Spanish. The other three media markets in this size category have fewer television stations. Only the Miami/Fort Lauderdale market had competition for cable service, which also is present in the top three markets [39]. The number of outlets decreased markedly between the three larger markets in this category and Wilkes Barre/Scranton (the 53rd- largest market).

We could not determine if this was due to a change in the number of outlets that can be supported between the 30th-largest market (Nashville) and the 53rd-largest market, the lack of a core urban area in Wilkes Barre/Scranton, or the relatively weak economy prevalent in Wilkes Barre/Scranton. See table 4 for the number of outlets in the large case study markets.

Table 4. Number of Outlets in the Largest City of the Large Markets—Miami/Fort Lauderdale, Charlotte, Nashville, and Wilkes Barre/Scranton

	Number of outlets			
Industry segment	Miami	Charlotte	Nashville	Scranton
Television stations	16	12	12	8
Radio stations	47	37	52	24
Daily newspapers	3	1	2	1

Source: GAO analysis of FCC data, Warren Online Cable and Television Factbook, and *Bowker's News Media Directory*.

Medium-Size Markets

The medium-size markets we analyzed are Tucson, Arizona (68); Springfield, Missouri (76); Chattanooga, Tennessee (86); Cedar Rapids/Waterloo/Iowa City/Dubuque, Iowa (89); and Myrtle Beach/Florence, South Carolina (105) [40]. Similar to the Miami/Fort Lauderdale market, the Tucson market has more television stations than the other case study markets in its size category, mainly because of the relatively large Hispanic population in this medium-size market. There are eight English-language television stations in Tucson, which is similar to the number in the other four medium-size markets. However, Tucson has a relatively large Hispanic population and therefore possesses a larger number of media outlets due to the presence of Spanish-language television and radio stations. Television markets which lack a dominant urban area and contain two or more large towns located some distance apart are often split into smaller radio markets [41]. The Cedar Rapids/Waterloo/Iowa City/Dubuque DMA contains three Arbitron radio markets and the Myrtle Beach/Florence DMA is split into two separate Arbitron radio markets. See table 5 for the number of outlets in the medium-size case-study markets.

Small Markets

The small markets we analyzed are Terre Haute, Indiana (151); Sherman, Texas/Ada, Oklahoma (161); Jackson, Tennessee (174); and Harrisonburg, Virginia (181) [42]. These small markets are characterized by significantly fewer media outlets—television stations, radio stations, and newspapers— than the larger markets. Table 6 illustrates the number of outlets in the small case study markets. Hence, for these markets, the conversion to digital broadcasting offers the possibility to improve the free, over-the-air choices to residents. Already, commercial television stations in Sherman/Ada and Harrisonburg use a second digital channel to provide the signal from a broadcast network that is not otherwise present in the market. For example, WHSV in Harrisonburg, an ABC affiliate, broadcasts the FOX network on one of the station's digital channels.

Table 5. Number of Outlets in the Largest City of the Medium-Size Markets— Tucson, Springfield, Chattanooga, Cedar Rapids/Waterloo/Iowa City/Dubuque, and Myrtle Beach/Florence

Industry segment	Number of outlets				
	Tucson	Springfield	Chattanooga	Cedar Rapids	Florence
Television stations	11	6	8	9	6
Radio stations	38	26	32	25	13
Daily newspapers	2	2	1	1	1

Source: GAO analysis of FCC data, Warren Online Cable and Television Factbook, and *Bowker's News Media Directory*.

Table 6. Number of Outlets in the Small Markets—Terre Haute, Sherman/Ada, Jackson, and Harrisonburg

Industry segment	Number of outlets			
	Terre Haute	Sherman/Ada	Jackson	Harrisonbur
Television stations	5	2	3	2
Radio stations	18	23	21	16
Daily newspapers	1	1	1	1

Source: GAO analysis of FCC data, Warren Online Cable and Television Factbook, and *Bowker's News Media Directory*.

Some Media Companies Participate in Operating Agreements

Some media companies participate in operating agreements that involve a partnership between two or more outlets. For example, some media companies participate in agreements to share content among several outlets. Other media companies participate in agreements wherein one company produces content or sells advertising through its own outlets and another company's outlets. These operating agreements are referred to, either by industry participants or FCC's rules, by a variety of names, including joint sales agreements, local marketing agreements, and time brokerage agreements [43] FCC's attribution rules—which seek to identify those interests in or relationships to licensees that have a realistic potential to affect the programming decisions of licensees or other core operating functions—apply to several types of operating agreements [44]. Additionally, the Newspaper Preservation Act of 1970 allows two competing newspapers in one community to merge some operations to help ensure the survival of both newspapers; the resulting arrangements are referred to as joint operating agreements [45].

In our 16 case study markets, we found several instances of media companies participating in operating agreements. We found these agreements in a variety of markets but not in the top three markets, suggesting that market size may influence the benefits that companies realize through such agreements. We found television stations participating in operating agreements in five markets—Nashville, Wilkes Barre/Scranton, Springfield, Myrtle Beach/Florence, and Terre Haute. In Springfield, there were two operating agreements between television stations and in Wilkes Barre/Scranton there were three operating agreements between television stations. We also found operating agreements between radio stations in Harrisonburg and Nashville. Finally, in Tucson, the two competing daily newspapers participate in a joint operating agreement.

In addition to formal operating agreements, media companies in a market often maintain informal content-sharing arrangements with each other. These most often cross different types of media, rather than occurring among competitors within the same industry segment. In our case study markets, we found a newspaper sharing articles with a television station; a newspaper sharing articles with a radio station in return for advertising spots; and a newspaper sharing journalists with a television station. In markets with common ownership of a radio or television station and a newspaper, such sharing of content and journalism resources occurred as a matter of course. We also found some contractual sharing of content between media outlets of the same type. Most often, one television station produced local news programs for other stations in the same market.

To some extent, these operating agreements may reduce the number of independent outlets. For example, in Wilkes Barre/Scranton, we identified eight television stations. However, one owner of two stations participated in an agreement with a third station. Additionally, the remaining four television stations participated in two separate agreements—each agreement covering two stations.

Thus, while there are eight television stations and seven owners in Wilkes Barre/Scranton, there are three loose commercial groupings in the market. Similarly, in Springfield, while there are six television stations, four stations participate in two separate agreements. This example suggests that the number of independently owned outlets in a given market might not always be a good indicator of how many independently produced local news or other programs are available in a market.

The Internet is Expanding Access to Media Content

The Internet delivers content from a virtually limitless supply of sources. For example, while residents of New York can read The New York Times, residents in Harrisonburg with access to the Internet also can read this publication. Most of the traditional media outlets—newspapers, radio stations, and television stations—in our case study markets maintain a Web site. This provides another means for residents to access the content of these outlets. However, we identified few news Web sites in our case study markets that were unaffiliated with the traditional media outlets. While there are many blogs and Web sites, when we spoke with stakeholders about assessing the number of "voices" in a media market, there was no consensus on how to count Internet outlets. Some stakeholders said that audience size was less important than the existence of many potential voices, while other stakeholders said that voices on the Internet mattered only when they reached an audience above a certain minimum size. Further, some stakeholders said that journalistic content was important, such as that arising from news gathering and investigations.

Ownership of Broadcast Outlets by Minorities and Women Appears Limited, but Comprehensive Data Are Lacking

While FCC collects data on the gender, race, and ethnicity of radio and television station owners every 2 years through its Ownership Report for Commercial Broadcast Stations, or Form 323, we found that these data have several weaknesses that undermine their usefulness for tracking and periodically reporting on the status of minority and women ownership. These weaknesses include (1) exemptions from filing for certain types of broadcast stations, such as noncommercial stations; (2) inadequate data quality procedures; and (3) problematic data storage and retrieval. Moreover, there are no other reliable government sources on the status of minority and women ownership. Nevertheless, the available evidence from industry stakeholders and experts we interviewed, as well as government and nongovernment reports, suggests that ownership of broadcast outlets by these groups is limited. We identified three primary barriers contributing to the limited levels of ownership by minorities and women These barriers include (1) the large scale of ownership in the media industry, (2) a lack of easy access to sufficient capital for financing the purchases of stations, and (3) the repeal of the tax certificate program, which provided financial incentives for incumbents to sell stations to minorities.

FCC Lacks Comprehensive Data on Ownership of Broadcast Outlets by Minorities and Women

Diversity has been a long-standing policy goal of FCC, including ownership by minorities and women. In 1998, FCC issued rules to collect data on the gender, race, and ethnicity of broadcast licensees. FCC decided to collect these data through its Annual Ownership Report, or Form 323. FCC noted that it was appropriate to develop "precise information on minority and female ownership of mass media facilities" and "annual information on the state and progress of minority and female ownership," thereby positioning "both Congress and the Commission to assess the need for, and success of, programs to foster opportunities for minorities and females to own broadcast facilities" [46] FCC began collecting these data in 1999.

The Form 323 is the only mechanism through which FCC collects information on the gender, race, and ethnicity of broadcast owners. FCC requires all commercial AM and FM radio stations and television stations to report the gender, race, and ethnicity of each owner with an attributable interest [47] on the Form 323. Owners and licensees must file the Form 323 every 2 years, whenever there is a transfer of control or assignment, or after the grant of a construction permit for a new commercial broadcast station.

As FCC's only information source on owners' gender, race, and ethnicity, the Form 323 data potentially could be used to determine and periodically report on the level of minority and women broadcast ownership. However we identified several weaknesses that limit the usefulness of the Form 323 data [48].

- *Filing exemptions.* Sole proprietors, partnerships, and noncommercial stations are not required to file the Form 323 [49]. Since the data from Form 323 do not include stations owned by sole proprietors, partnerships, or noncommercial stations, it is not possible to use the Form 323 data to identify either the full universe of broadcast stations owned by minorities and women or the number of minority and women owners. FCC also does not require the filing of the Form 323 for low-power stations.
- *Data quality procedures.* According to FCC officials, FCC does not verify or periodically review the gender, race, and ethnicity data submitted on the Form 323. According to these officials, a staff person from FCC's Video Division reviews submitted Form 323s and this staff person focuses on ensuring compliance with the commission's multiple ownership and citizen ownership rules. These officials told us that station owners were responsible for determining the accuracy of their Form 323 submissions. Should an error be found by the owner, FCC requires the owner to submit an additional Form 323.
- *Data storage and retrieval.* Companies must file the Form 323 electronically. However, FCC allows owners to provide attachments with their electronic filing of the Form 323. These attachments may include the gender, race, and ethnicity data. Since these data are not entered into the database, the data are unavailable for electronic query. Of further concern, the database retains all submitted Form 323s, even forms that contain incorrect information and have since been updated with a corrected Form 323. Thus, any aggregation or summary of the Form 323 records through electronic query is unreliable according to FCC officials.

FCC has taken some steps to address concerns with the Form 323 data, but overall some weaknesses remain. According to FCC officials, FCC added an amendment process to the Form 323 interface, thereby allowing owners to modify information on a previously submitted Form 323. FCC also put in place edit checks that preclude owners from skipping questions, including questions on the owners' gender, race, and ethnicity. However, FCC still allows attachments for Form 323s to be submitted and has no regular review mechanism for these attachments to determine if the owners provided correct information biennially as required. Moreover, there are no consequences for misfiling that would encourage accurate, complete, and timely submission of the Form 323. On December 18, 2007, FCC adopted a Notice of Proposed Rulemaking that seeks comment on how the commission can best improve its collection of data regarding the gender, race, and ethnicity of broadcast licensees [50].

Ownership of Broadcast Outlets by Minorities and Women Appears Limited

While reliable government data on ownership by minorities and women are lacking, ownership of broadcast outlets by these groups appears limited. According to the industry stakeholders and experts we interviewed, the level of ownership by minorities and women is limited. Recent studies generally support this conclusion. Three reports commissioned by FCC as part of its broadcast ownership proceeding found relatively limited levels of ownership of television and radio stations by minorities and women. Further, in a 2006 report, Free Press found that for full-power television stations, women and minority ownership was about 5 percent and 3 percent, respectively [51]. Specifically, the report noted that women owned a majority stake in 67 of 1,349 full-power commercial television stations and minorities owned 44 stations, 9 of which were owned by one company. In another report, Free Press estimated that women owned approximately 629 of 10,506 (or 6 percent) of full-power radio stations and minorities owned 812 stations (or 8 percent) of full- power radio stations [52].

Minorities and Women Encounter a Variety of Barriers to Ownership of Broadcast Outlets

According to prior government reports and industry stakeholders and experts we interviewed, three factors help explain the relatively small percentages of minority and women broadcast owners.

Scale of ownership. In 2000, FCC and the National Telecommunications and Information Administration (NTIA) released separate reports suggesting that the current scale of ownership had been detrimental for minority and women ownership of broadcast outlets. In 2000, FCC commissioned a report that found industry deregulation in 1996 and the resulting consolidation had produced significant barriers to new entry and to the viability of small, minority- and women-owned companies [53]. The report cited inflated station prices and disparate advertising revenues. NTIA's report included similar observations about the impact of consolidation on station prices and advertising revenue [54].

Industry representatives and experts we interviewed also identified the scale of ownership as a barrier for minorities and women. Thirty-six of 56 interviewees who mentioned barriers to ownership reported that the consolidation of broadcast ownership had been detrimental for minority and women ownership. According to these industry representatives and experts, the scale of current ownership mattered in several important ways. First, few stations are made available for purchase, limiting opportunities for the entry of new owners, such as minorities and women. Second, incumbent owners may prefer to trade stations with other incumbent owners rather than sell stations. Given the limited ownership by minorities and women today, trading does little to expand their ownership. Third, when stations become available for sale, investors and other financing entities prefer multiple station purchases rather than single station purchases in order to capture economies of scale. Like trading, such transactions favor incumbent companies that are well- established over new entrants such as minorities and women. Lastly, the scale of the industry affects the viability of current and prospective minority and women owners, since these owners must often compete with large conglomerate owners with sizable market share and greater resources.

Access to capital. Both FCC's and NTIA's reports on minority and women ownership also included discussion and findings on the role of capital and the lack thereof for minorities and women. According to FCC's commissioned report, access to capital was the barrier most often cited by study participants. The report found that banks often repeatedly rejected minority broadcast owners as applicants for a variety of reasons, ranging from racial discrimination to a lack of familiarity with the industry on the part of the bank. Similarly, NTIA's report noted the importance of access to capital and described public and private sources of financing for minorities and women. The report concluded that despite these sources, access to capital continued to be a key concern.

Industry stakeholders and experts we interviewed also mentioned the importance of access to capital and financing and the challenge it presents to minority and women ownership. Thirty-five of 56 interviewees reported that a lack of access to capital impeded greater entry by minorities and women into the broadcast industry. In particular, these industry representatives and experts described two ways in which the barrier posed by a lack capital is compounded by the nature of station sales and FCC rules. First, since stations generally do not advertise their properties for sale, individuals and companies looking to purchase a station must have cash on hand. Prospective buyers cannot wait for an announced sale and then acquire financing. This is a challenge for minority and women broadcasters, who often lack information on upcoming station sales and generally have fewer financial resources. Second, sellers are deterred from working with buyers who lack capital since any equity remaining in the station would be considered attributable interest under FCC's rules. Retaining attributable interest in one property could make it difficult for these owners to buy different properties in the same market, due to FCC's local ownership limits. Consequently, sellers would forgo working with prospective buyers who lack readily available capital rather than assume any risk to potential future acquisitions.

Repeal of the tax certificate program. From 1978 to 1995, FCC operated a tax certificate program under section 1071 of the Internal Revenue Code that provided for the seller of a broadcast station to defer capital gains taxes on the sale if the station was sold to a minority-owned company. In 1995, the Congress repealed this program. During this period, FCC issued a total of 328 tax certificates for use in broadcast station transactions (285 for radio station sales and 43 for television station sales).

Both FCC's and NTIA's reports on minority and women ownership cited the importance of the tax certificate as an incentive for incumbent broadcast owners to advertise and work with prospective minority buyers.

FCC's commissioned report described the tax certificate program as the "single most effective program in lowering market entry barriers and providing opportunities for minorities to acquire broadcast licenses in the secondary market" [55].

NTIA's report also found that the program fostered minority ownership. Many experts we interviewed also agreed that this program was important for promoting minority ownership. Twenty-five of 56 stakeholders we interviewed said that the elimination of the tax certificate program was a factor in the current limited level of minority- owned broadcast stations.

A Variety of Economic, Legal and Regulatory, and Technical Factors Influence Media Ownership

Economic factors—including high fixed costs and the size of the market—influence the number of media outlets available in markets, the presence of operating agreements between outlets, and incentives for firms to consolidate their operations. Legal and regulatory factors appear to influence ownership of media outlets as well, by constraining the number and types of media outlets that a single entity can own. Lastly, technological factors, such as the emergence of the Internet, appear to facilitate entry by allowing entry with limited investment; however stakeholders' opinions varied on the significance of these entrants on media markets.

High Fixed Costs and Local Market Size Are Important Economic Factors that Influence the Number and Ownership of Media Outlets

We found that fixed costs are prevalent in the media industry and are an important economic factor influencing the number and ownership of media outlets. Fixed costs refer to those costs that do not change with the number of units produced or sold. Fifty-two of 102 stakeholders we interviewed mentioned that high fixed costs are a factor influencing media ownership, and the academic literature also highlighted the importance of fixed costs. For example, in broadcast network television, two stakeholders reported that the fixed costs of producing 1 hour of programming range from $3 million to $5 million—regardless of how many viewers the programming attracts. Similarly for newspapers, the costs of purchasing a printing press and producing and editing news stories are not very sensitive to the number of copies a newspaper produces or sells. Stakeholders also reported high fixed costs for radio and television stations, cable television, and DBS.

The size of the local market also is an important economic factor influencing the number and ownership of media outlets, since market size broadly determines an outlet's potential for generating advertising revenues. For example, several stakeholders reported that although the costs of operating television and radio stations are similar regardless of market size, smaller markets have smaller audiences and fewer local advertisers for station operators to pursue. Accordingly, stakeholders reported that owners are less likely to sell stations in large markets than in smaller markets. According to data from Bear, Stearns and Company, Inc., 4 of the 137 television station transactions announced in the first two quarters of 2007 involved stations broadcasting in the top three markets. Conversely, stakeholders representing a large radio group owner and a national television broadcaster both reported that their companies are currently selling stations in smaller markets.

Both high fixed costs and market size have implications for the number of outlets in a given market, the presence of operating agreements between outlets, and incentives for firms to consolidate their operations in local and national markets.

- *Number of outlets*. Market size and fixed costs influence the number of outlets in a market. The size of the market broadly determines the advertising revenues available to outlets in the market. In addition, costs in the media industry do not vary considerably between large and small markets. Therefore, large markets can generally support more outlets than small markets. Twenty-six interviewed stakeholders mentioned that the size of the market influences the number of outlets available, and 10 stakeholders reported that markets with larger populations and advertising revenues can support more media outlets and owners than smaller markets. For example, in New York—the largest market—we identified 21 television stations and 15 separate owners for those stations. In contrast, in Harrisonburg, Virginia—the smallest market in our review— we identified only 2 broadcast television stations and 2 separate owners, one of which was a public television station. Similarly, in the newspaper industry, several stakeholders reported that most newspaper markets can support only one daily newspaper because of high fixed costs in the industry. Accordingly, 9 of the 16 markets we evaluated had one daily newspaper, and 4 markets supported two newspapers [56].

- *Operating agreements*. The size of a local market and high fixed costs produce incentives for media outlets to enter into operating agreements with other local outlets. Specifically, we found that outlet owners in markets with smaller advertising revenues have incentives to enter into operating agreements with other outlets to spread fixed costs across multiple outlets to maximize their profitability. Thirty interviewed stakeholders reported that the size of the market can influence the need for such operating agreements. In our case study analyses, we identified 9 operating agreements between 17 television stations in 5 markets [57]. We found these arrangements in a variety of markets, but not in the top three markets. It appears that medium-size markets are better suited to these arrangements than small markets because they offer a larger pool of potential outlet partners than would be available in smaller markets. Furthermore, two stakeholders reported that these agreements may increase the number of outlets available in a market by helping weaker stations remain in operation and by bringing new broadcasting networks into a market.
- *Local and national consolidation*. The combination of high fixed costs and market size also encourages media consolidation both within local markets and nationwide. Because competition for advertising revenues among radio and television broadcast stations occurs at the local level, nine stakeholders representing television, radio, and newspaper companies reported that their industries have incentives to consolidate operations across multiple outlets to reduce their fixed costs and claim a larger share of available advertising revenues. For example, six

stakeholders reported that owning multiple stations in a local market allows a single owner to program its stations with diverse formats to reach a larger share of local listeners and provide multiple channels for advertisers. Media firms likewise have incentives to seek economies of scale and consolidate their operations nationally. For example, stakeholders reported that the cable industry has consolidated in recent years to cluster local systems into wider regional networks to reach larger audiences and serve a wider range of advertisers. Stakeholders also reported that serving a wider network of subscribers gives cable operators greater leverage in negotiating agreements to carry programming produced by broadcast and cable television networks. In the newspaper industry, one national newspaper company reported that it publishes almost 1,000 nondaily newspapers across the country, which enables the company to offer flexible advertising packages to national and local advertisers.

Stakeholder Perspectives Vary on the Influence of Legal and Regulatory Factors on Media Ownership

In addition to economic factors, several legal and regulatory policies appear to have influenced media ownership, including local television and radio station ownership limits, the newspaper-broadcast cross ownership ban, and the 1996 Act. However, stakeholder perspectives varied on the extent to which the individual policies may have influenced current ownership.

- *Local television and radio station ownership limits.* FCC's rules limit the number of radio stations, television stations, and combinations of radio and television stations that a single entity can own; as such, the rules influence the ownership of these media outlets. Twenty-three of 29 industry stakeholders we spoke with cited either the local radio or television limits as a factor influencing the ownership of media outlets. Several stakeholders reported that the local television ownership limit—which permits ownership of two television stations in larger markets—allows over-the-air television stations to better compete with other media outlets, including cable television and DBS providers, which have significantly more channels and air time to sell advertising. Several other stakeholders reported that this rule would be more beneficial if it were permitted in smaller markets to preserve struggling outlets, rather than in large markets where advertising revenues are greater. With regard to radio, several industry stakeholders reported that the local ownership caps limit consolidation in markets where companies were operating at the ownership limits.

- *Newspaper-broadcast cross ownership ban.* By limiting the markets where a single entity can have common ownership of a daily newspaper and a broadcast outlet, FCC's rules affect the ownership of these media outlets. Stakeholders from three companies with newspaper holdings reported that the potential synergies and economic benefits to cross-ownership are overstated; two stakeholders reported that differences between television and newspaper cultures and products limit collaboration between the two platforms. On the other hand, three companies owning both newspapers and television stations in the same market reported that cross-ownership offers synergies such as improved sharing of resources and information between outlets. Similarly, stakeholders from two companies indicated that cross-ownership has helped their outlets produce more in-depth, local news than they would otherwise be able to provide.
- *Telecommunications Act of 1996.* The 1996 Act loosened restrictions on the ownership of radio stations—allowing greater ownership of local radio stations and eliminating nationwide limits on ownership of radio stations. Twenty of 45 nonbusiness stakeholders, such as academics, industry associations, and think tanks, identified the 1996 Act as a factor influencing media ownership; 9 of 57 business stakeholders similarly identified the 1996 Act. Three stakeholders reported that the changes in the 1996 Act brought capital, business expertise, and content diversity to the radio industry, as new entrants sought to invest in underfunded radio stations. Alternatively, several other stakeholders reported that the 1996 Act resulted in overconsolidation in the radio industry, as many small operators were bought out by conglomerate owners.

Technological Factors Appear to Facilitate New Entry

New technologies appear to facilitate entry, thereby promoting new content and competition. In particular, the Internet provides new opportunities for individual citizens and companies to produce their own Internet publications with little investment. For example, individuals and companies no longer need to acquire a broadcast license and invest in broadcast facilities to distribute content to a wide audience. Forty-four stakeholders told us that the Internet creates an abundance of outlets, while only 17 disagreed. The Pew Internet & American Life Project, an Internet-focused research center, found that in 2003, "more than 53 million American adults had used the Internet to publish their thoughts, respond to others, post pictures, share files and otherwise contribute to the explosion of content available online." Additionally, 67 of 102 stakeholders mentioned competition from new entrants from the Internet or new telecommunications services as a factor influencing media ownership. For example, six newspaper industry stakeholders reported that industry revenues have suffered from the availability of low-cost or free classified advertising services available on the Internet.

While many stakeholders reported that the Internet creates an abundance of outlets, opinions varied as to the significance of these example, several stakeholders cited increases in the number of outlets available on the Internet, such as blogs, but said there is little evidence that these outlets are widely read or are journalistic substitutes for newspapers. Similarly, several other stakeholders estimated that a significant portion of the content available on these Web sites originates from large, established media firms such as newspapers.

Stakeholders' Opinions Varied on Modifications to Media Ownership Rules, but Business Stakeholders Were More Likely to Favor Deregulation

The stakeholders we interviewed seldom agreed on proposed modifications to media ownership rules. However, most business stakeholders expressing opinions on these rules were more likely to report that they should be relaxed or repealed. In contrast, nonbusiness stakeholders who expressed opinions on the rules were more likely to report that the rules should be left in place or strengthened. Both business and nonbusiness stakeholders who expressed an opinion on the previously repealed tax certificate program supported either reinstating or expanding the program to encourage the sale of broadcast outlets to minorities.

- *Newspaper-broadcast cross-ownership ban.* As mentioned earlier, on December 18, 2007, FCC modified its rules to permit common ownership of a daily newspaper and broadcast outlet in some markets. Prior to FCC's action, the stakeholders we spoke with were fairly evenly divided on whether FCC should modify its rule prohibiting cross-ownership of newspapers and broadcast outlets in the same local area. Of the 50 stakeholders expressing an opinion on the matter, 27 reported that the rule should be repealed and 23 said that the rule should either be left as is or strengthened. However, among business and nonbusiness stakeholders interviewed, there were clear differences in opinion on this issue. Fourteen of 20 nonbusiness stakeholders were in favor of strengthening or leaving the rule in place. In contrast, 21 of 30 business stakeholders were in favor of repealing the regulation. For example, 13 of 14 stakeholders from multisector media companies stated the rule should be repealed.

- *Local television and radio ownership limits.* Stakeholders were fairly evenly divided on whether FCC should alter rules limiting the number of broadcast television and radio stations a single entity can own in a local market. Of the 50 stakeholders expressing an opinion on the matter, 27 said that the rules should be repealed and 23 said that the rule should either be left as is or strengthened. However, opinions within stakeholder segments were more consistent. Fourteen of 19 nonbusiness stakeholders were in favor of strengthening or leaving the rules in place, while 22 of 31 business stakeholders were in favor of repealing the regulations.
- *National television ownership cap.* The majority (65 of 102) of stakeholders expressed no opinion on this issue. Of the 37 who did express an opinion, 22 said that the cap should be left as is or lowered, further restricting ownership, while 15 favored raising or repealing the cap. But these results differed for nonbusiness and business stakeholders. Whereas 11 of 15 nonbusiness stakeholders stated that the cap should be left as is or lowered, further restricting ownership, 11 of 22 business stakeholders indicated that the cap should raised or repealed.
- *Reinstitution of minority tax certificate program.* Of the 102 stakeholders interviewed, most (72) expressed no opinion as to whether the minority tax certificate program should be reinstated. However, among the 30 stakeholders who mentioned this issue, there was broad consensus in favor of reinstating some version of this program. Twenty-eight of these 30 stakeholders indicated that the program should be either reintroduced without changes or expanded, and 2 said that the program was not needed and should not be reinstated.

CONCLUSION

The media serve an important function in American life through their role in disseminating news, information, and entertainment. Though media options vary by local market, the overall growth in the communications industry and the emergence of the Internet have provided unprecedented levels of media choices to the American public. At the same time, economic forces appear to encourage local and national consolidation and operating agreements that reduce the number of independent voices. Moreover, though smaller owners, including minorities and women, have opportunities to enter the media industry by way of Internet-based and niche publications, these groups continue to face long-standing challenges to the ownership of radio and television stations. Since 1999, FCC has collected data on the gender, race, and ethnicity of radio and television station owners. In undertaking this effort, FCC noted that it was appropriate to develop "precise information on minority and female ownership of mass media facilities" and "annual information on the state and progress of minority and female ownership," thereby positioning "both Congress and the Commission to assess the need for, and success of, programs to foster opportunities for minorities and females to own broadcast facilities." Yet, data weaknesses stemming from how the data are collected, verified, and stored limit the benefits of this effort. Further, more accurate and reliable data would allow FCC to better assess the impact of its rules and regulations and would enable the Congress to make more informed legislative decisions about issues such as whether to reinstate the tax certificate program. While FCC recently adopted a Notice of Proposed Rulemaking regarding its data on broadcaster licensee gender, race, and ethnicity, this process has only recently begun and its outcome is unclear.

Recommendation for Executive Action

To more effectively monitor and report on the ownership of broadcast outlets by minorities and women, we recommend that the Chairman, FCC, identify processes and procedures to improve the reliability of FCC's data on gender, race, and ethnicity so that these data can be readily used to accurately depict the level, nature, and trends in minority and women ownership, thereby enabling FCC and the Congress to determine how well FCC is meeting its policy goal of diversity in media ownership.

Agency Comments

We provided a draft of this report to FCC for its review and comment. FCC provided technical comments that we incorporated where appropriate. FCC did not provide comments on our recommendation. FCC's written comments appear in appendix IV.

As agreed with your office, unless you publicly announce the contents of this report earlier, we plan no further distribution until 30 days from the date of this letter. At that time, we will send copies of this report to the appropriate congressional committees and to the Chairman of the Federal Communications Commission. We will also make copies available to others upon request. In addition, the report will be available at no charge on the GAO Web site at http://www.gao.gov.

If you or your staff have any questions about this report, please contact me at (202) 512-2834 or heckerj@gao.gov. Contact points for our Offices of Congressional Relations and Public Affairs may be found on the last page of this report. Contact information and major contributors to this report are listed in appendix V.

Sincerely yours,

JayEtta Z. Hecker
Director, Physical Infrastructure Issues

Appendix I: Scope and Methodology

To assess the current ownership of media outlets, we used a case study methodology. The case studies consisted of the largest city in 16 Nielsen Designated Market Areas (DMA). To select the case study DMAs, we used a stratified random sample. We obtained the 2007 list of DMAs from the Nielsen Media Research Web site. We stratified the DMAs by size and randomly selected four large, four medium-size, and four small markets for the case study analysis. We defined large markets as those with 500,000 to 3 million households; medium-size markets as those with 150,000 to 499,999 households; and small markets as those with fewer than 150,000 households. In addition to the 12 random selections, we selected the top three markets (New York, Los Angeles,

Chicago) as a separate take-all stratum and selected Tucson as a test market in which to count outlets because of its large Hispanic population.

Within each market, we counted the number of television stations, radio stations, newspapers, and multichannel video programming distributors (MVPD) and the owners of these outlets. We considered outlets available to residents in the largest city to avoid counting multiple outlets not present throughout the market; outlets not counted primarily consist of weekly suburban newspapers not published in the largest city. Below we discuss our approach to counting television stations, radio stations, newspapers, and multichannel video programming distributors.

Television stations. We used the Warren Television and Cable Factbook: Online to count the number of full-power television stations located in each market. We included both commercial and noncommercial full-power television stations in our count of stations. We used company Web sites and ownership data that stations filed with the Federal Communications Commission (FCC) through its Form 323 to determine the ownership of the station. For commercial stations, we counted the owner as the ultimate legal entity on whose behalf the ownership was registered with FCC. This provided an accurate count of group ownership, as well as identified any multiple station ownership within a single market.

Radio stations. We first determined the largest city located within each television market. Some selected case study markets had multiple core cities; we used Miami for the Miami/Fort Lauderdale DMA, Scranton for the Wilkes Barre/Scranton DMA, Florence for the Myrtle Beach/Florence DMA, and Cedar Rapids for the Cedar Rapids/Waterloo/Iowa City/Dubuque DMA. We used FCC data to determine the number of full-power commercial and noncommercial radio stations located within close listening distance of the city [1]. Due to its large geographic area and sparse population, we identified the four most populous counties in the Sherman/Ada DMA and determined the number of radio stations located within 20 miles of the largest town in each county [2] We adopted this approach because the market is too small to have an Arbitron radio market [3]. The Sherman/Ada market also is located between the Oklahoma City and Dallas/Fort Worth markets, so we used an atlas to ensure that the radio stations located within 20 miles of Ada, Oklahoma, and Sherman, Texas, both located on the geographical edge of the DMA, were physically located inside the Sherman/Ada DMA.

Our methodology produced counts of radio stations that may not match the actual number of full-power radio stations located in a DMA for one or both of the following reasons. First, the DMA may contain more than one Arbitron radio market, such as in the Cedar Rapids/Waterloo/Iowa City/Dubuque DMA and we counted radio stations from only one radio market. Second, the DMA is geographically large and the number of full- power commercial and noncommercial radio stations located within close listening distance of the core city does not capture all of the radio stations.

Newspapers. We used Bowker's News Media Directory to identify the daily, weekly, ethnic, religious, and special interest publications whose area of dominant influence included the core urban area. We counted daily and weekly newspapers separately and combined the ethnic, religious, and special interest publications into the "other" category. We also surveyed Web sites of the major daily newspapers in the core urban area of each of our case study markets to determine if there were any additional publications not contained in Bowker's News Media Directory. We also used the directory from the New American Media organization to identify additional ethnic publications available in New York, Los Angeles, Chicago, Miami, Charlotte, Nashville, and Chattanooga [4]. This source did not list publications for the other case study markets. Fieldwork in the Nashville and Tucson markets turned up additional publications that were missing in our data source. Our data sources likely undercount small local weeklies and other types of independent journals.

Multichannel video programming distributors. We obtained the list of cable operators in each state from FCC's database of registered cable operators (http://www.fcc.gov/mb/engineering/liststate.html). We used the Warren Television and Cable Factbook to verify that a cable company listed in the FCC database provided service in the core urban area. If the market contained more than one urban area, we used the largest city (e.g., Miami). In addition to cable companies, we included both direct broadcast satellite companies (DirecTV and Echo Star). The minimum MVPD count a market could have with this methodology is three. Any number greater than three reflects the presence of a cable overbuilder or a telecommunications company that is offering subscription television services in the core urban area of the DMA.

In addition to case studies, we reviewed the relevant literature and conducted interviews to assess the current ownership of media outlets. We identified studies through a general literature review. We interviewed agency officials at FCC and the National Telecommunications and Information Administration (NTIA) about media ownership policies. We also identified 102 stakeholders in academia, think tanks, nonprofits, and media companies and interviewed them to obtain their views on FCC's ownership policies and issues affecting media ownership. We used the same structured interview for all interviewees and analyzed the content of the interview responses. To ensure consistent analysis of the interview responses, we had two reviewers independently apply the content analysis tool to each interview write-up and standardized the coding to ensure reliability. We cross-tabulated the interview content to determine patterns in responses and the extent to which interview subjects supported particular positions.

To identify the economic, legal and regulatory, and technological factors affecting media ownership, we reviewed the relevant literature, studies, and regulations and conducted interviews. We obtained and analyzed data on the radio and television industries from Bear, Stearns and Company, Inc. We obtained data from the Census Bureau's 2006 American Community Survey to study the economic and demographic characteristics of households in the metropolitan statistical area around the central city in each case study DMA. We obtained data on the average household effective buying income for each DMA from the Television Bureau of Advertising for all 210 DMAs; we also obtained the list of top 25 Hispanic, African-American, and Asian media markets from the bureau. We reviewed the relevant economic literature and studies on media ownership. We reviewed relevant legislation and FCC notices, orders, and reports to assess legal factors. We also obtained information on economic, legal and regulatory, and technological factors from industry stakeholders as part of the structured interview process.

To describe the levels of minority and women ownership of broadcast outlets, to identify factors that help explain these levels, and to assess FCC's data collection efforts, we reviewed relevant reports, interviewed agency officials and industry stakeholders, and analyzed FCC's forms and processes. To describe the levels of minority and women ownership of broadcast outlets, and factors affecting their ownership, we interviewed industry stakeholders, FCC and NTIA officials, and members of FCC's Advisory Committee on Diversity for Communications in the Digital Age. We also reviewed relevant reports prepared by or for FCC, NTIA, and nongovernment organizations (such as Free Press). To determine FCC's data collection efforts, we reviewed the relevant regulatory forms (such as FCC's Form 323), and FCC documents and commissioned reports. Additionally, we interviewed FCC officials responsible for collecting the Commission's data on broadcast ownership about the completeness and quality of the information in their databases. Because of inadequacies in the FCC ownership data, evidence suggesting limited ownership of media outlets by minorities and women comes from stakeholder opinions, as well as studies commissioned by FCC and prepared by NTIA and nongovernment organizations.

We conducted this performance audit from February 2007 through March 2008 in accordance with generally accepted government auditing standards. Those standards require that we plan and perform the audit to obtain sufficient, appropriate evidence to provide a reasonable basis for our findings and conclusions based on our audit objectives. We believe that the evidence obtained provides a reasonable basis for our findings and conclusions based on our audit objectives.

Appendix II: Results from Case Study Locations

To study the nature and level of media ownership, we randomly selected 12 case study markets, including 4 from each of three market strata— large, medium, and small. In addition, we selected the three largest markets as a separate stratum and judgmentally selected an extra market from the medium stratum (Tucson) to test our methodology for data collection and structured interviews. Information about the markets we selected for case study analysis appears in table 7. These media markets account for about 20 percent of all television households in the United States. For information about our methodology for counting outlets in each media market, see appendix I.

The Three Largest Media Markets

New York, New York (1)

The New York City designated market area (DMA) is the largest media market in the United States, with over 7 million households. This media market comprises 13 counties in northern New Jersey, 1 county in southwest Connecticut, 1 county in northeastern Pennsylvania, and 14 counties in New York, including all those on Long Island and the five boroughs. The New York City DMA is the largest African-American media market, the second-largest Asian media market, and the second-largest Hispanic media market in the United States. In terms of average household disposable income, [1] the New York City DMA ranks fourth highest in the United States, making it a very attractive market for a broadcast media outlet.

The four major networks (ABC, CBS, FOX, and NBC) own and operate their local broadcast television affiliates in New York. (In smaller television markets, the major networks are less likely to own and operate their local affiliates).

Table 7. Local Media Markets Selected for Analysis

2007 Nielsen size rank	Designated market area	Number of TV households	Percentage of U.S. market	Stratum
1	New York, N.Y.	7,366,950	6.616	Very Large
2	Los Angeles, Calif.	5,611,110	5.039	Very Large
3	Chicago, Ill.	3,455,020	3.103	Very Large
16	Miami-Ft. Lauderdale, Fla.	1,538,620	1.382	Large
26	Charlotte, N.C.	1,045,240	0.939	Large
30	Nashville, Tenn.	944,100	0.848	Large
53	Wilkes Barre-Scranton, Pa.	590,170	0.530	Large
70	Tucson (Sierra Vista), Ariz.	433,310	0.389	Medium
76	Springfield, Mo.	402,310	0.361	Medium
86	Chattanooga, Tenn.	347,380	0.312	Medium
89	Cedar Rapids-Waterloo-Iowa City & Dubuque, Iowa	333,270	0.299	Medium
105	Myrtle Beach-Florence, S.C.	272,340	0.245	Medium
151	Terre Haute, Ind.	144,880	0.130	Small
161	Sherman-Ada, Tex., Okla.	124,330	0.112	Small
174	Jackson, Tenn.	95,070	0.085	Small
181	Harrisonburg, Va.	87,630	0.079	Small

Source: GAO analysis of Nielsen 2007 television ratings data.

One company owns three television stations, all of which broadcast in Spanish. There are seven noncommercial Public Broadcasting Service (PBS) affiliates, several independent stations, and three Spanish-language network affiliates among the remaining broadcast television stations. The owners of radio outlets in the New York media market include several large national media companies with five or six outlets each and 28 entities with a single outlet in the market. Therefore, about two-thirds of the owners in the New York City DMA are operating a single radio outlet [2]. The majority of the radio stations in this market broadcast in English, several broadcast in Spanish, and one broadcasts in Cantonese. In the aggregate, the 73 radio stations in the New York media market provide listeners with a wide variety of content.

Table 8. Numbers of Outlets and Owners by Media Sector for the New York City DMA

Industry segment	Number of outlets	Number of owners
Broadcast television	21	15
Radio	73	44
Newspaper[a]		
Daily	5	5
Weekly	41	18
Other[b]	177	136
Multichannel video program	4	4

Source: GAO analysis of FCC data, Warren Online Cable and Television Factbook, and *Bowker's News Media Directory*.

[a]Reflects availability in New York City. In addition to those newspapers identified by Bowker's, we found 51 other newspapers listed for New York City in the online version of the National Ethnic Media Directory, but were not able to identify the ownership for all of the newspapers. These 51 newspapers are not included in the table because of this.

[b]Includes data for specialty publications, religious newspapers, and ethnic newspapers.

[c]Three cable companies operate in New York City, but their service territories do not overlap. A representative household has one of these companies available plus an overbuilder (i.e., a competing cable company in a market formerly licensed exclusively to another cable company) and both satellite television companies, DirecTV and EchoStar.

There is more cross-ownership of newspapers and broadcast outlets in the New York market than in other media markets, but there is also more diversity in specialty publications. News Corporation owns The Wall Street Journal, The New York Post, and two broadcast television stations (WWOR and WNYW); The New

York Times Company owns The New York Times daily newspaper and a radio station (WQXR); and Tribune Company owns one Spanish-language daily newspaper (Hoy) and one television station (WPIX). New York is the center of the publishing industry in the United States and far more specialty publications are located here than in other media markets.

Los Angeles, California (2)

The Los Angeles DMA is the second-largest media market in the United States, with over 5.6 million households. It includes eight counties in southern California and stretches from the Pacific Coast east to Nevada. The Los Angeles DMA is the largest Hispanic media market, the largest Asian media market, and the sixth-largest African-American media market in the United States. This media market ranks 24th in the nation for average household disposable income, the lowest ranking among the three largest media markets.

The four major networks (ABC, CBS, FOX, and NBC) own and operate their local broadcast television affiliates in the Los Angeles DMA, just as they do in the New York City DMA. One of these networks owns three stations in this market while two other networks each own two stations. Los Angeles has more broadcast television stations than New Yorkstations broadcast in Spanish and there are two Asian-language stations in Los Angeles.

Table 9. Numbers of Outlets and Owners by Media Sector for the Los Angeles DMA

Industry segment	Number of outlets	Number of owners
Broadcast television	24	19
Radio[a]	69	34
Newspaper[b]		
Daily	2	2
Weekly	15	5
Other[c]	73	59
Multichannel video program[d]	4	4

Source: GAO analysis of FCC data, Warren Online Cable and Television Factbook, and *Bowker's News Media Directory.*

The Los Angeles DMA is the largest radio market in the country. According to advertising data for 2005, radio stations in the Los Angeles DMA [3] competed for over $1 billion of advertising revenue, exceeding the advertising revenue for the next largest (New York) and the third-largest (Chicago) radio advertising markets by over $200 million and about $500 million, respectively. The Los Angeles DMA is somewhat more concentrated: one owner has reached the FCC cap of eight stations and another is close to the cap with seven stations. By contrast, no radio station owner in New York has reached the eight-station cap. Fewer stations are operated by a single owner in Los Angeles (20) than in New York (28), yet over half the Los Angeles station owners (about 59 percent) operate a single station. The large number of radio stations in Los Angeles provides a wide variety of content, and about a quarter of the stations broadcast in a language other than English, including 13 in Spanish, 3 in Korean, and 2 in Chinese. Stations located in Mexico and in neighboring U.S. media markets can also be heard in all or portions of the Los Angeles DMA, enhancing the market's diversity.

Fewer newspapers are located in Los Angeles than in the New York DMA, yet the number is still large compared with other media markets. There is one instance of cross-ownership: Tribune Company owns the Los Angeles Times and a broadcast television station (KTLA) in this market.

Chicago, Illinois (3)

The Chicago DMA is the third-largest media market in the United States, with over 3.4 million households. It contains 11 counties in northern Illinois and 5 counties in northwest Indiana.

Chicago is the third-largest African-American media market, the fifth-largest Asian market, and the fifth-largest Hispanic media market in the United States. The Chicago DMA has the seventh-highest average household income in the nation. The Chicago DMA has eight fewer broadcast television stations than the Los Angeles DMA; there are four fewer Spanish-language, no Asian- language, and three fewer independent English-language stations in Chicago. The Chicago DMA also has five fewer television stations than the New York DMA. Radio outlet ownership is similar to that in Los Angeles— there are 2 owners that operate seven stations each in this market. Radio ownership is characterized by a few companies operating near the FCC ownership limit while 27 of the 38 owners (or 71 percent) own and operate a single radio station.

Chicago has one instance of cross-ownership—under a waiver from FCC, Tribune Company owns two daily newspapers, the Chicago Tribune and Hoy, a Spanish-language daily; a television station, WGN; and a radio station, WGN-AM, in this media market.

Table 10. Numbers of Outlets and Owners by Media Sector for the Chicago DMA

Industry segment	Number of outlets	Number of owners
Broadcast television	16	13
Radio	65	38
Newspaper[a]		
Daily	3	3
Weekly	17	11
Other[b]	52	47
Multichannel video program distributor[c]	4	4

Source: GAO analysis of FCC data, Warren Online Cable and Television Factbook, and *Bowker's News Media Directory*.

[a]Reflects availability in the city of Chicago. In addition to the newspapers in the listed sources, we found 35 other newspapers listed for Chicago in the online version of the National Ethnic Media Directory, but were not able to identify the owners of all of them. These 35 newspapers are not included in the table because of this.

[b]Includes data for specialty publications, religious newspapers, and ethnic newspapers. [c]Two cable companies operate in the city of Chicago, but their service territories do not overlap. A representative household has one of these companies available plus an overbuilder and both satellite television companies.

Large Media Markets

After the top three markets, we defined large media markets as those with between 500,000 and 3 million households. There are 59 media markets in this size category, ranging from Philadelphia (4) to Tulsa (62). We randomly selected four of these markets for case study analysis.

Miami/Fort Lauderdale, Florida (16)

The Miami/Fort-Lauderdale DMA includes 1.5 million households, making it the 16th-largest media market in the nation. It is the 3rd-largest Hispanic media market in the United States, after New York and Los Angeles; the 10th-largest African-American media market; and the 23rd-largest Asian media market. The average household disposable income for the DMA ranks 33rd in the nation, yet the advertising revenue for radio ranks 11th.

Although the Miami/Fort Lauderdale DMA has about 2 million fewer households than the Chicago DMA, both markets support 16 broadcast television outlets. In Miami, these include affiliates of the eight primary English-language commercial networks, [4] five Spanish-language stations, and three public television stations. Three of the English-language affiliates are owned and operated by two of the four major television networks. Commercial television stations that are owned and operated by the major networks are characteristic of our large case study media markets. Sixteen, or two-thirds, of the radio station owners operate a single outlet in the Miami/Fort Lauderdale DMA—the same proportion as in the New York City DMA. One company owns seven radio stations.

This city supports two Spanish-language daily newspapers in addition to the English-language newspaper. Among the other newspapers available to residents are several Spanish-language weeklies and an African-Americanfocused weekly.

Table 11. Numbers of Outlets and Owners by Media Sector for the Miami/FortLauderdale DMA

Industry segment	Number of outlets	Number of owners
Broadcast television	16	13
Radio	47	24
Newspaper[a]		
Daily	3	2
Weekly	5	5
Other[b]	10	10
Multichannel video program	4	4

Source: GAO analysis of FCC data, Warren Online Cable and Television Factbook, and Bowker's News Media Directory.

[a]Reflects availability in Miami. In addition to the newspapers in the listed sources, we found 14 other newspapers listed for Miami in the online version of the National Ethnic Media Directory, but were not able to identify the ownership for all of them. These 14 newspapers are not included in the table because of this.

[b]Includes data for specialty publications, religious newspapers, and ethnic newspapers.

[c]One cable company operates in Miami. A representative household has this company available plus a telephone company offering digital cable and both satellite television companies.

Charlotte, North Carolina (26)

Charlotte is the 26th-largest media market in the United States, with over 1 million households. It is the 16th-largest African-American media market, but is not among the top 25 Hispanic or Asian media markets in the United States.

The broadcast television market here includes a higher percentage of noncommercial stations and more duopolies—one company owning two stations—than do the case study media markets described thus far. Specifically, 4 of the DMA's 12 broadcast television stations, or 33 percent, are noncommercial and are affiliated with PBS. Among the 8 commercial television stations, there are two duopolies, and 2 of the noncommercial PBS stations have one owner, a local university. All of the commercial stations broadcast in English, meaning that residents in this DMA who desire media content in languages other than English must subscribe to a cable or satellite television service.

In terms of radio advertising revenue, Charlotte is the 29th-largest market. Fewer radio stations are located within listening distance of the core city limits than in Miami or Nashville. Ownership of radio outlets is more concentrated in Charlotte than in the larger markets. There are 17 owners, including 1 large national media company that owns 7 radio stations in this market and 10 commercial and noncommercial owners that each operates a single station in the market.

Table 12. Numbers of Outlets and Owners by Media Sector for the Charlotte DMA

Industry segment	Number of outlets	Number of owners
Broadcast television	12	9
Radio	37	17
Newspaper[a]		
Daily	1	1
Weekly	0	0
Other[b]	11	11
Multichannel video program distributor[c]	3	3

Source: GAO analysis of FCC data, Warren Online Cable and Television Factbook, and *Bowker's News Media Direct*ory.

[a]Reflects availability in the city of Charlotte. In addition to the newspapers in the listed sources, we found five other newspapers listed for Charlotte in the online version of the National Ethnic Media Directory, but were not able to identify the owners of all of them. These five newspapers are not included in the table because of this.

[b]Includes data for specialty publications, religious newspapers, and ethnic newspapers.

[c]One cable company operates in the city of Charlotte. A representative household has this company available plus both satellite television companies.

Nashville, Tennessee (30)

The Nashville DMA is the 30th-largest media market in the United States, with over 940,000 households. Covering 49 counties in Tennessee and Kentucky, this DMA covers a wide geographic area. Nashville is not among the top 25 media markets for African Americans, Asians, or Hispanics. In terms of average household disposable income, the DMA ranks 43rd among all media markets in the United States, and it ranks lower for television advertising revenue than for population size.

Two of the Nashville DMA's 12 broadcast television stations are noncommercial public television stations. One company owns 2 of the commercial broadcast television stations and has a local service agreement to run a third station with another outlet owner. All 12 television stations broadcast in English.

Table 13. Numbers of Outlets and Owners by Media Sector for the Nashville DMA

Industry segment	Number of outlets	Number of owners
Broadcast television	12	11
Radio	52	35
Newspaper[a]		
Daily	2	2
Weekly	4	3
Other[b]	9	9
Multichannel video program distributor[c]	3	3

Source: GAO analysis of FCC data, Warren Online Cable and Television Factbook, and *Bowker's News Media Directory*.

[a]Reflects availability in Nashville. In addition to the newspapers in the listed sources, we found one other newspaper listed for Nashville in the online version of the National Ethnic Media Directory. Since we could not identify the ownership for all of the newspapers found in the National Ethnic Media Directory, we did not include them in the case study market count tables.

[b]Includes data for specialty publications, religious newspapers, and ethnic newspapers.

[c]One cable company operates in the city of Nashville. A representative household has this company available plus both satellite television companies.

With 52 radio outlets, Nashville has more radio stations than Miami, Charlotte, and Wilkes Barre/Scranton, the other three case study media markets in our large-size category, and radio ownership is much less concentrated. Twenty-four, or 69 percent, of the station owners operate a single station in this market;

two companies own five stations each and the remaining nine companies own the rest. One of the group owners with five radio stations also has a joint sales agreement with a radio station owned by another company in Nashville.

Wilkes Barre/Scranton, Pennsylvania (53)

The Wilkes Barre/Scranton DMA covers 17 counties in northeastern Pennsylvania and is the 53rd-largest media market in the country, with over 590,000 households. This DMA is unusual in that it has no large core city, but rather a series of large- and medium-size towns located in the valleys of this mountainous region. The DMA ranks 148th in the nation for average household disposable income.

With about 350,000 fewer households than the Nashville DMA, the Wilkes Barre/Scranton DMA also has fewer broadcast television stations and radio stations. The DMA contains seven commercial stations, all of which are broadcast network affiliates, and one PBS affiliate. There are no full- power independent television stations in this media market.

Table 14. Numbers of Outlets and Owners by Media Sector for the Wilkes Barre/Scranton DMA

Industry segment	Number of outlets	Number of owners
Broadcast television	8	7
Radio[a]	24	14
Newspaper[b]		
Daily	1	1
Weekly	1	1
Other[c]	4	3
Multichannel video program distributor[d]	3	3

Source: GAO analysis of FCC data, Warren Online Cable and Television Factbook, and *Bowker's News Media Directory*.

[a]includes all stations identified by FCC data at or within 20 miles of Scranton, the largest town in this DMA. Does not include stations that rebroadcast the signal of another radio station.

[b]Reflects availability in Scranton.

[c]includes data for specialty publications, religious newspapers, and ethnic newspapers.

[d]One cable company operates in the city of Scranton. A representative household has this company available plus both satellite television companies.

Difficulties in the local economy—and a television advertising market that, according to industry sources we spoke with, is smaller than warranted for a DMA of its population size—have encouraged cost-sharing arrangements between the commercial broadcast television stations. Two of the stations have a single owner, and this owner has a local service agreement with a third station. Two other stations have a local service agreement under which they share everything except programming and finances. The remaining two commercial television stations have a joint sales agreement. Thus, the seven commercial television stations in this DMA operate in three loose commercial groupings. Ten of the 14 owners of radio outlets in the Wilkes Barre/Scranton DMA, or 71 percent, own and operate a single radio station in the market. One company owns five stations, another owns four stations, and two companies own the remaining five stations. Because of the mountainous terrain in this DMA, rebroadcasting of other stations' signals occurs frequently.

Medium-Size Media Markets

After the top three markets and large markets, we defined medium-size media markets as those containing from 150,000 to 499,999 households. There are 86 media markets in this size category, ranging from Lexington (63) to Salisbury (148). We randomly selected 4 of these markets for case study analysis. In addition, before making our random selection, we judgmentally selected the Tucson, Arizona, DMA as a test market for our data collection and structured interview methodology because of its large Hispanic population.

Tucson, Arizona (70)

The Tucson DMA is the 70th-largest media market in the United States, containing over 433,000 households. It is also the 25th-largest Hispanic media market in the United States, with over 115,000 Hispanic households. This DMA ranks 74th for average household disposable income.

The Tucson DMA includes six commercial television stations affiliated with English-language networks, three commercial television stations affiliated with Spanish-language networks, and two public television stations. There are two duopoly owners of commercial stations—one of English-language stations and one of Spanish-language stations.

Radio outlet ownership is relatively concentrated in Tucson, with one media company operating six radio stations in this market and two media companies operating five stations each. In total, 7 owners operate more than one station and 10 owners, or 59 percent, operate a single station in the market.

The Tucson DMA has two daily newspapers, the *Arizona Daily Star* and the *Tucson Citizen*. They operate together under a joint operating agreement allowed by the Newspaper Preservation Act of 1970.

Table 15. Numbers of Outlets and Owners by Media Sector for the Tucson DMA

Industry segment	Number of outlets	Number of owners
Broadcast television	11	8
Radio	38	17
Newspaper[a]		
Daily	2	2
Weekly	2	2
Other[b]	5	5
Multichannel video program distributor[c]	3	3

Source: GAO analysis of FCC data, Warren Online Cable and Television Factbook, and Bowker's News Media Directory.

[a]Reflects availability in the city of Tucson.

[b]Includes data for specialty publications, religious newspapers, and ethnic newspapers.

[c]One cable company operates in the city of Tucson. A representative household has this company available plus both satellite television companies.

Springfield, Missouri (76)

The Springfield, Missouri, DMA includes 31 counties in Missouri and Arkansas and is the 76th-largest media market in the country, with just over 402,000 households. In terms of average household disposable income, this DMA ranked 183rd out of 210 media markets in the United States. Five commercial television broadcasting stations and one public broadcasting television station serve this DMA. Two of the commercial television stations have a local service agreement under which they share everything in their business operations except programming and finances, and another two commercial stations operate together under a shared service agreement.

Five companies own 20 radio outlets, including two companies with 5 radio stations each. Six owners each operate a single radio station in this market. One company controls the primary daily newspaper in the DMA and one of the weeklies in Springfield itself.

Table 16. Numbers of Outlets and Owners by Media Sector for the Springfield DMA

Industry segment	Number of outlets	Number of owners
Broadcast television	6	6
Radio	26	11
Newspaper[a]		
Daily	2	2
Weekly	1	1
Other[b]	2	2
Multichannel video program distributor[c]	3	3

Source: GAO analysis of FCC data, Warren Online Cable and Television Factbook, and Bowker's News Media Directory.

[a]Reflects availability in the city of Springfield.

[b]Includes data for specialty publications, religious newspapers, and ethnic newspapers.

[c]One cable company operates in the city of Springfield. A representative household has this company available plus both satellite television companies.

Table 17. Numbers of Outlets and Owners by Media Sector for the Chattanooga DMA

Industry segment	Number of outlets	Number of owners
Broadcast television	8	8
Radio	32	20
Newspaper[a]		
Daily	1	1
Weekly	2	1
Other	0	0
Multichannel video program distributor[b]	3	3

Source: GAO analysis of FCC data, Warren Online Cable and Television Factbook, and Bowker's News Media Directory.

[a]Reflects availability in the city of Chattanooga. In addition to the newspapers in the listed sources, we found one other newspaper listed for Chattanooga in the online version of the National Ethnic Media Directory. Since we could not identify the ownership for all of the newspapers found in the National Ethnic Media Directory, we did not include them in the case study market count tables.

[b]One cable company operates in the city of Chattanooga. A representative household has this company available plus both satellite television companies.

Chattanooga, Tennessee (86)

The Chattanooga DMA covers 17 counties in Tennessee, Georgia, and North Carolina; includes over 347,000 households; and is the 86th-largest media market in the United States. This market supports six commercial television broadcasting stations, all affiliated with a commercial network, and two public television broadcasting stations. Five radio outlet owners control 17 radio stations, including two owners that control 4 stations each. Fifteen owners, or 75 percent, each operate a single station. There is no cable overbuilder in this DMA.

Cedar Rapids/Waterloo/Iowa City/Dubuque, Iowa (89)

The Cedar Rapids/Waterloo/Iowa City/Dubuque DMA includes 21 counties in Iowa, contains over 333,000 households, and is the 89th-largest media market in the country. Like the Wilkes Barre/Scranton DMA, the Cedar Rapids/Waterloo/Iowa City/Dubuque DMA does not contain a single core urban area. However, unlike the Wilkes Barre/Scranton DMA, this DMA is subdivided among three radio markets. To ensure comparability with other case study media markets, we counted stations located in the Cedar Rapids radio market because Cedar Rapids has the largest population of the four towns.

The Cedar Rapids/Waterloo/Iowa City/Dubuque DMA supports more broadcast television outlets than comparably populated media markets. There are six affiliates of national broadcast networks, two public television stations, and one independent television station, all of which broadcast in English. Two large national radio companies own 6 radio stations each, and 6 of the 11 radio outlet owners in the DMA, or 55 percent, each operate a single radio station. There is one daily newspaper in Cedar Rapids.

Myrtle Beach/Florence, South Carolina (105)

The Myrtle Beach/Florence DMA consists of eight counties in South Carolina and southeastern North Carolina. With over 272,000 households, this DMA is the 105th-largest media market in the United States, and in terms of average household disposable income, it ranks 176th out of 210 media markets. This television market DMA contains two medium-size towns that are geographically separated. Florence is the more populous of the two, so we counted the radio stations and newspapers located in this town.

The Myrtle Beach/Florence media market has six broadcast television outlets and five owners. The duopoly owner is an educational association that operates two public television stations. Two commercial television stations operate under a local marketing agreement that enables them to share fixed operating costs.

Table 18. Numbers of Outlets and Owners by Media Sector for the Cedar Rapids DMA

Industry segment	Number of outlets	Number of owners
Broadcast television[a]	9	8
Radio[b]	25	11
Newspaper[c]		
Daily	1	1
Weekly	0	0
Other	0	0
Multichannel video program distributor[d]	3	3

Source: GAO analysis of FCC data, Warren Online Cable and Television Factbook, and Bowker's News Media Directory.

[a]includes all broadcast television outlets whose signal reaches Cedar Rapids, the largest city in the DMA. Does not include one full-power broadcast television station in Dubuque whose signal does not reach Cedar Rapids.

[b]Includes all radio outlets within 20 miles of Cedar Rapids. includes all newspapers located in Cedar Rapids.

[d]One cable company operates in the city of Cedar Rapids. A representative household has this company available plus both satellite television companies

In the Florence radio market (the larger of the two radio markets in the Myrtle Beach/Florence DMA), there are four owners of a single station and two group owners. One group station owner controls five stations in this market, while the other controls four stations.

Small Media Markets

The smallest media markets are those with fewer than 150,000 households. There are 61 media markets in this size category, ranging from Palm Springs, California (149), to Glendive, Montana (210). We randomly selected 4 of these markets for case study analysis.

Terre Haute, Indiana (151)

The Terre Haute DMA includes five counties in eastern Illinois and nine counties in western Indiana. There are fewer than 145,000 households in this market, making it the 151st-largest media market, and in terms of average household disposable income, it ranks 174th out of 210 media markets.

Table 19. Numbers of Outlets and Owners by Media Sector for Florence

Industry segment	Number of outlets	Number of owners
Broadcast television	6	5
Radio[a]	13	6
Newspaper[b]		
Daily	1	1
Weekly	1	1
Other	0	0
Multichannel video program distributor[c]	3	3

Source: GAO analysis of FCC data, Warren Online Cable and Television Factbook, and Bowker's News Media Directory.

[a]Based on FCC data for full-power radio stations located at or within 20 miles of Florence.

[b]Based on data for Florence.

[c]One cable company operates in the city of Florence. A representative household has this company available plus both satellite television companies.

Table 20. Numbers of Outlets and Owners by Media Sector for the Terre Haute DMA

Industry segment	Number of outlets	Number of owners
Broadcast television	5	5
Radio	18	11
Newspaper[a]		
Daily	1	1
Weekly	0	0
Other[b]	1	1
Multichannel video program distributor[c]	3	3

Source: GAO analysis of FCC data, Warren Online Cable and Television Factbook, and Bowker's News Media Directory.

[a]Reflects availability in the city of Terre Haute.

[b]Includes data for specialty publications, religious newspapers, and ethnic newspapers.

[c]Two cable companies operate in the city of Terre Haute, but their service territories do not overlap. A representative household has one of these companies available plus both satellite television companies.

Three commercial television stations and two public television stations operate in this market. Two of the commercial stations operate under a joint operating agreement that allows them to share operating costs. As noted, cost-sharing arrangements also existed in the other four case study markets where we found a large difference between the population rank and the average household disposable income rank. Three owners operate 10 radio stations in this market, including two owners that operate 4 stations each, and eight owners each operate a single radio station in this market.

Sherman, Texas/Ada, Oklahoma (161)

The Sherman/Ada DMA contains 10 counties in southern Oklahoma and 1 county in northern Texas. Sherman is the largest community within this media market, with about 37,000 residents. This media market contains just over 124,000 households and is the 161st-largest media market. This market contains a higher proportion of Native American residents than any of our other case study markets.

Although there are two broadcast television stations in this market, there is no public television station. The two commercial stations are local affiliates of two different major broadcast networks, and one of these stations carries a third major broadcast network on its second digital signal. Residents of this DMA who own a digital television thus have free access to three of the four major broadcast networks.

Table 21. Numbers of Outlets and Owners by Media Sector for the Sherman/Ada DMA

Industry segment	Number of outlets	Number of owners
Broadcast television	2	2
Radio	23	13
Newspaper[a]		
Daily	1	1
Weekly	0	0
Other	0	0
Multichannel video program distributor[b]	3	3

Source: GAO analysis of FCC data, Warren Online Cable and Television Factbook, and Bowker's News Media Directory.

[a]Based on data for Sherman, Texas.

[b]One cable company operates in the city of Sherman. A representative household has this company available plus both satellite television companies.

While a distinct television market, the Sherman/Ada DMA does not constitute a separate radio market [5]. Six owners operate more than one radio station in this market, including one owner that operates four stations and two owners (one of whom is the Chickasaw Nation) that operate three stations each. Seven owners each operate a single radio station in this market.

Jackson, Tennessee (174)

The Jackson DMA includes the town of Jackson and six counties in Tennessee to the east and northeast of Memphis. With just over 95,000 households, this media market is the 174th-largest in the nation. The DMA has two commercial broadcast television stations, both of which are local affiliates of major networks, and one public television station.

Neither of the two commercial television stations broadcasts a second major network on its second digital signal. Five radio station owners operate more than one station, including two companies that operate four stations each and another that operates three stations in this market. Six owners each operate a single radio station in this market.

Table 22. Numbers of Outlets and Owners by Media Sector for the Jackson DMA

Industry segment	Number of outlets	Number of owners
Broadcast television	3	3
Radio	21	11
Newspaper[a]		
Daily	1	1
Weekly	0	0
Other	0	0
Multichannel video program distributor[b]	4	4

Source: GAO analysis of FCC data, Warren Online Cable and Television Factbook, and Bowker's News Media Directory.

[a]Based on data for Jackson.

[b]Two cable companies operate in the city of Jackson. A representative household has a choice between one of these companies or both satellite television companies.

Harrisonburg, Virginia (181)

With just over 87,000 households, thc Harrisonburg DMA is the smallest media market we selected for case study analysis.

Located northwest of Richmond, this DMA is the 181st-largest media market in the country and comprises two counties in Virginia and one county in West Virginia.

This market contains one commercial television station and one public television station. The commercial television station is an affiliate of a major broadcast network for its analog signal, but it broadcasts programming from two other broadcast networks and its analog affiliate on its digital signals. Residents of this DMA who have a digital television thus have free access to the programming of three broadcast networks.

Four radio station owners operate more than one station, including one company that operates five stations and another that operates four stations in this media market. Three owners each operate a single station in this market.

Table 23. Numbers of Outlets and Owners by Media Sector for the Harrisonburg DMA

Industry segment	Number of outlets	Number of owners
Broadcast television	2	2
Radio	16	7
Newspaper[a]		
Daily	1	1
Weekly	0	0
Other	0	0
Multichannel video program distributor[b]	3	3

Source: GAO analysis of FCC data, Warren Online Cable and Television Factbook, and Bowker's News Media Directory.

[a]Based on data for Harrisonburg.

[b]One cable company operates in the city of Harrisonburg. A representative household has this company available plus both satellite television companies.

Appendix III: Organizations and Individuals Interviewed

We conducted interviews with the following individuals and representatives from the following organizations.

Table 24. Organizations and Individuals Interviewed

Access Tucson
AfraGenesis Communications
The Alliance for Community Media
American Women in Radio and Television, Inc.
C. Edwin Baker, University of Pennsylvania Law School
Bear, Stearns & Co. Inc.
Belo Corp.
Brewer Broadcasting
Carolyn M. Byerly, Howard University
Angela J. Campbell, Georgetown University Law Center
Capitol Broadcasting Company, Inc.
CBS Corporation
Chattanooga Times Free Press
Citadel Broadcasting Corporation
The City Paper (Nashville, Tennessee)
Clear Channel Communications, Inc.
Clear Channel Communications, Inc. (Tucson, Arizona, radio stations)
Comcast Corporation
Benjamin Compaine, Northeastern University
Consumer Federation of America
Consumers Union
Council Tree Communications, Inc.
Cox Enterprises, Inc.
Cumulus Media Inc. (Nashville, Tennessee, radio stations)
Democracy Now!
DIRECTV
EchoStar Communications Corporation
FCC Advisory Committee on Diversity for Communications in the Digital Age
Fisher Communications, Inc.
Free Press
Future of Music Coalition
Gannett Company, Inc.
Juan Gonzalez, New York Daily News columnist
James T. Hamilton, Duke University
Thomas W. Hazlett, George Mason University School of Law
Hubbard Broadcasting Inc.
Independent Film & Television Alliance
Independent Press Association
Journal Broadcast Group (Tucson, Arizona, radio and television stations)
JPMorgan Chase & Company

Table 24. (Continued)

Michael L. Katz, University of California, Berkeley
KHRR (Tucson, Arizona, television station)
KMSB, KTTU (Tucson, Arizona, television stations)
KTTB-FM (Edina, Minnesota, radio station)
KUAT (Tucson, Arizona, television station)
KVOA (Tucson, Arizona, television station)
KWBA (Tucson, Arizona, television station)
KXCI (Tucson, Arizona, radio station)
Mark Lloyd, Center for American Progress
Robert W. McChesney, University of Illinois at Urbana-Champaign
The McClatchy Company
Media Access Project
Media General, Inc.
Minority Media and Telecommunications Council
Philip M. Napoli, Fordham University School of Business
Nashville Community Newspaper Alliance
Solidus Co., NashvillePost.com
National Association for Multi-Ethnicity in Communications
National Association of Black Owned Broadcasters
National Association of Broadcasters
National Cable and Telecommunications Association
National Federation of Community Broadcasters
National Hispanic Media Coalition
National Telecommunications and Information Administration
NBC Universal
News Corporation
Newspaper Association of America
The Newspaper Guild-Communications Workers of America
The New York Times Company
Nexstar Broadcasting Group, Inc.
Eli M. Noam, Columbia University
NRG Media
Bruce M. Owen, Stanford University
Parents Television Council
Pennsylvania Public Television Network
The Philadelphia Daily News
The Philadelphia Inquirer
Project for Excellence in Journalism
Prometheus Radio Project
Prudential Financial, Inc.

Publishers of Tucson, Arizona, area newspapers: Tucson Weekly, Inside Tucson Business, The Daily Territorial, Vail Sun (Wick Communications), Explorer, and DesertLeaf
The Pulse (Chattanooga, Tennessee)
Reclaim the Media
LaVonda N. Reed-Huff, Syracuse University School of Law
The Seattle Times Company
ShootingStar Broadcasting, WZMY-TV (Derry, New Hampshire)
Sinclair Broadcasting Group, Inc.
South Central Radio Group, WJXA, WCJK (Nashville, Tennessee, radio stations)
Adam D. Thierer, The Progress and Freedom Foundation
Time Warner, Inc.
Times-Shamrock Communications
Tribune Company
Tucson Citizen
Joel Waldfogel, The Wharton School, University of Pennsylvania
The Walt Disney Company
The Washington Post Company
WDEF, WDOD (Chattanooga, Tennessee, radio stations)
Steven S. Wildman, Michigan State University
Women in Cable Telecommunications
WSMV (Nashville, Tennessee, television station)
WTCI (Chattanooga, Tennessee, television station)
WTVC (Chattanooga, Tennessee, television station)
WTVF (Nashville, Tennessee, television station)
XM Satellite Radio, Inc.
Young Broadcasting, Inc.

APPENDIX IV: COMMENTS FROM THE FEDERAL COMMUNICATIONS COMMISSION

Federal Communications Commission
Washington, D.C. 20554

February 15, 2008

Ms. JayEtta Z. Hecker
Director, Physical Infrastructure Issues
United States Government Accountability Office
Washington, D.C. 20548

Re: GAO-08-383

Dear Ms. Hecker:

Here are our comments on a draft copy of GAO-08-383, "Economic Factors Influence the Number of Media Outlets in Local Markets, While Ownership by Minorities and Women Appears Limited and Is Difficult to Assess." The report examines the current state of media ownership and recommends that the Commission take steps to improve the reliability of its data on the gender, race, and ethnicity of broadcast outlet owners. It also concludes that, while there are weaknesses in the Commission's current data, ownership of broadcast outlets by women and minorities appears limited.

Strengthening the diverse and robust marketplace of ideas that is essential to our democracy has long been a fundamental Commission goal. I would like to emphasize, as the report acknowledges, that on December 18, 2007, the Commission adopted a *Report and Order and Third Further Notice of Proposed Rulemaking*, which includes several measures designed to foster participation in the broadcasting industry by new entrants and small businesses, including minority- and women-owned businesses, by expanding ownership opportunities and increasing access to capital. For example, the item:

- Affords eligible entities – an entity that would qualify as a small business consistent with Small Business Administration ("SBA") standards for its industry grouping, based on revenue that acquire an expiring construction permit, additional time to build out the facility;
- Modifies the Commission's equity/debt plus attribution standard, to facilitate investment in eligible entities;
- Encourages local and regional banks to participate in SBA-guaranteed loan programs to facilitate broadcast and telecommunications-related transactions.
- The item also specifically seeks comment on methods for enhancing the accuracy and reliability of data collection on the gender, race, and ethnicity of broadcast licensees. The Commission will take appropriate action after reviewing the comments received.

I would also like to make a few observations concerning the report's description of the rules governing ownership of broadcast outlets adopted by the Commission on December 18, 2007. First and foremost, while the report states that the Commission "adopted several revisions to its media ownership rules," only the rule banning newspaper/broadcast cross-ownership was, in fact, revised. The Commission retained all other rules as they currently are in effect. Moreover, the report fails to note that applicants seeking to overcome a negative presumption about a proposed newspaper/broadcast combination need to demonstrate by clear and convincing evidence that post-merger, the merged entity will increase the diversity of independent news outlets (e.g., separate editorial and news coverage decisions) and increase competition among independent news sources in the relevant market. The Commission will use the following factors to inform its evaluation: (1) the level of concentration in the DMA; (2) a showing that the combined entity will significantly increase the amount of local news in the market; (3) a showing that the newspaper and the broadcast outlets each will continue to employ its own news and editorial staff and that each will exercise its own independent news judgment; and (4) the financial condition of the newspaper or broadcast station in the proposed combination, and if the newspaper or station is in financial distress, the proposed owner's commitment to invest significantly in newsroom operations.

Second, the 39 percent national television ownership cap is statutory, having been enacted as part of the Consolidated Appropriations Act, 2004. Similarly, the numerical limits contained in the local radio ownership rule track the numerical limits passed by Congress in the Telecommunications Act of 1996.

Thank you for the opportunity to comment on the draft report.

Sincerely,

for Monica Desai
Chief, Media Bureau

REFERENCES

[1] Telecommunications Act of 1996, Pub. L. No. 104-104, 110 Stat. 56, Section 202(h).

[2] *Prometheus Radio Project v. FCC*, 373 F.3d 372 (3rd Cir. 2004), cert. denied, 545 U.S. 1123 (2005). The court had earlier stayed FCC's rules and continued the stay during the review of the rules on remand. The court, in rehearing, lifted its stay of a portion of the rules that pertained to the methodology used to define local radio markets

[3] GAO, *Telecommunications: Preliminary Information on Media Ownership, GAO-08-330R (*Washington, D.C.: Dec. 14, 2007).

[4] According to Nielsen, a DMA consists of all counties whose largest viewing share is given to stations of the same market area. There are 210 nonoverlapping DMAs that cover the entire continental United States, Hawaii, and parts of Alaska.

[5] These markets are Miami/Fort Lauderdale, Florida (the 16th largest market); Charlotte, North Carolina (26); Nashville, Tennessee (30); Wilkes Barre/Scranton, Pennsylvania (53); Springfield, Missouri (76); Chattanooga, Tennessee (86); Cedar Rapids/Waterloo/Iowa City/Dubuque, Iowa (89); Myrtle Beach/Florence, South Carolina (105); Terre Haute, Indiana (151); Sherman, Texas/Ada, Oklahoma (161); Jackson, Tennessee (174); and Harrisonburg, Virginia (181).

[6] These markets are New York, New York (1); Los Angeles, California (2); and Chicago, Illinois (3).

[7] This market is Tucson, Arizona (70).

[8] We did not review whether the agreements fell within the requirements of FCC's attribution rules

[9] To prepare its reports, Free Press relied on data from FCC—including its database and Form 323 filings—and BIA Media Access Pro. The Free Press findings of relatively limited levels of ownership by minorities and women are generally consistent with the findings in three studies commissioned by FCC and a 2000 NTIA report. We did not evaluate the reliability of the Free Press reports

[10] *2006 Quadrennial Regulatory Review – Review of the Commission's Broadcast Ownership Rules and Other Rules Adopted Pursuant to Section 202 of the Telecommunications Act of 1996,* Report and Order and Order on Reconsideration, FCC 07-216, 2008 FCC LEXIS 1083 (released Feb. 4, 2008).

[11] *The Commission's Cable Horizontal and Vertical Ownership Limits*, Fourth Report and Order and Further Notice of Proposed Rulemaking, FCC 07-2 19, 2008 FCC LEXIS 1254 (released Feb. 11, 2008).

[12] "FCC Adopts Rules to Promote Diversification of Broadcast Ownership," FCC News Release, 2007 LEXIS 9663, Dec. 18, 2007.

[13] *Broadcast Localism*, Report on Broadcast Localism and Notice of Proposed Rulemaking, FCC 07-218, 2008 FCC LEXIS 809 (released Jan. 24, 2008).

[14] See FY 2004 Consolidated Appropriations Act, Pub. L. No. 108-199, 118 Stat. 3 et seq., Section 629.

[15] "Grade B" is an FCC-defined measure of signal strength pertaining to the availability of an over-the-air signal with a rooftop antenna.

[16] There is no limit on the number of AM or FM radio stations that a single entity can own nationwide. See Pub. L. No. 104-104, 110 Stat. 56, Section 202(a)(c).

[17] For purposes of this rule, major media voices include major newspapers and full-power television stations.

[18] There are two limited circumstances in which this negative presumption would be reversed: (1) the newspaper or broadcaster is failed or failing or (2) the proposed transaction results in a new source of a significant amount of local news in a market.

[19] Similar to Grade B contour, "Grade A" contour is a measure of signal strength, but is generally a smaller geographic area than the Grade B contour

[20] Newspaper-broadcast combinations that predate imposition of the existing ban are permitted. Companies also may seek a waiver from FCC to permit a newspaper-broadcast combination.

[21] For purposes of this rule, media voices include independently owned and operating full- power television stations, radio stations, daily newspapers with a circulation that exceeds 5 percent of the households in the DMA, one cable system if that system is generally available to households in the DMA, and independently owned out-of-market radio stations with a minimum share as reported by Arbitron.

[22] *Time Warner Entertainment Co. v. FCC, 240* F3d 1126 (D.C. Cir. 2001).

[23] In addition to full-power television stations, there were approximately 568 Class A and 2,227 low-power television stations in 2006.

[24] In addition to full-power radio stations, there were approximately 770 low-power FM stations in 2006.

[25] Thus, nearly 95 million households subscribed to an MVPD service in 2006. By way of comparison, according to Nielsen Media Research, there were approximately 111 million television households in 2006.

[26] *See Implementation of Section 3 of the Cable Television Consumer Protection and Competition Act of 1992, Statistical Report on Average Prices for Basic Service, Cable Programming Services, and Equipment*, 21 FCC Rcd 15087 (2006).

[27] *Revi ew of the Syndication and Financial Interest Rules*, 10 FCC 12165 (1995).

[28] Each of these companies owns television stations that reach more than 20 percent of the nation's television households.

[29] See *Annual Assessment of the Status of Competition in the Market for the Delivery of Video Programming,* 21 FCC Rcd 2503 (2006) (FCC 06-11).

[30] DBS companies DirecTV and EchoStar have approximately 16.0 and 13.1 million subscribers, respectively, placing these companies in the top 4 MVPD providers with Comcast and Time Warner.

[31] These two separate companies are controlled by National Amusement

[32] On Nov. 13, 2007, FCC granted, subject to conditions, Clear Channel's application to assign its television stations to Newport Television LLC, which is wholly owned by affiliates of Providence Equity Partners, Inc

[33] According to the 2006 American Community Survey, nonwhite households account for 36 percent of households in the New York City metropolitan statistical area (MSA), 43 percent in the Los Angeles MSA, and 31 percent in the Chicago MSA.

[34] Disposable income refers to effective buying income—a bulk measurement of market potential indicating the ability to buy. Average household effective buying income figures are from the Television Bureau of Advertising.

[35] We defined a cable overbuilder as a second cable system competing directly with an incumbent cable operator.

[36] For example, WZRC 1480 AM in New York broadcasts in Cantonese, WNVR 1030 AM in Chicago broadcasts in Polish, and KYPA 1230 AM in Los Angeles broadcasts in Korean

[37] The Tribune Company owns a daily newspaper and one or more broadcast outlets in both Los Angeles and Chicago. News Corporation owns two television stations and a daily newspaper in New York.

[38] We defined large media markets as those containing between 500,000 and 3 million households.

[39] The Charlotte, Nashville, and Wilkes Barre/Scranton markets do not have cable competition.

[40] We defined medium-size media markets as those containing between 150,000 and 500,000 households.

[41] We are using the Nielsen DMA for the case study analyses. In some instances, a geographically large DMA is split up into several smaller Arbitron radio markets.

[42] We defined small media markets as those containing fewer than 150,000 households

[43] Under FCC's attribution rules, a time brokerage agreement (also know as a local marketing agreement) is the sale by a licensee of discrete blocks of time to a "broker" that supplies the programming to fill that time and sell the commercial spot announcements in it. A joint sales agreement is an agreement with a licensee of a "brokered station" that authorizes a "broker" to sell advertising time for the "brokered station." See 47 C.F.R. 73.3555.

[44] We did not review whether the agreements fell within the requirements of the attribution rules. The attribution rules determine what interests are cognizable under FCC's broadcast ownership rules; the attribution rules are not ownership limitations in themselves. These rules impose an affirmative obligation on licensees to determine whether a particular agreement is attributable and, if it is, to file the agreement with FCC.

[45] The Newspaper Preservation Act of 1970 requires written consent of the Attorney General of the United States for future joint operating arrangements. Prior to granting such approval, the Attorney General shall determine that not more than one of the newspaper publications involved in the arrangement is a publication other than a failing newspaper, and that approval of such arrangement would effectuate the policy and purpose of the Act. See 15 U.S.C. Section 1801 et seq.

[46] *1998 Biennial Regulatory Review—Streamlining of Mass Media Applications, Rules, and Processes; Policies and Rules Regarding Minority and Female Ownership of Mass Media Facilities;* Report and Order, 13 FCC Rcd. 23056, 23096-23097 (1998).

[47] The gender, race, and ethnicity of owners with attributable interest must be provided on a station's Form 323. FCC defines each officer, director, and owner of stock accounting for 5 percent or more of the issued and outstanding voting stock of a corporation as having an attributable interest. Where the 5 percent stock owner is itself a corporation, each of its stockholders, directors, and "executive" officers (president, vice president, secretary, treasurer, or their equivalents) is considered a holder of an attributable interest, unless an exhibit establishing that an individual director or officer will not exercise authority or influence in areas that will affect the corporate respondent or the station is submitted.

[48] For its broadcast ownership proceeding, FCC commissioned three studies assessing the status of minority and women broadcast ownership; all three studies explored the adequacy of FCC's Form 323 data records and found the aggregate data to be unreliable.

[49] Noncommercial stations are required to file a Form 323-E, which does not collect data on gender, race, or ethnicity.

[50] "FCC Adopts Rules to Promote Diversification of Broadcast Ownership," FCC News Release, Dec. 18, 2007.

[51] Free Press, *Out of the Picture: Minority & Female TV Station Ownership in the United States* (Washington, D.C., October 2006).

[52] Free Press, *Off the Dial: Female and Minority Radio Station Ownership in the United States* (Washington, D.C., June 2007)

[53] Ivy Planning Group LLC, *Who's Spectrum Is It Anyway?: Historical Study of Market Entry Barriers, Discrimination and Changes in Broadcast and Wireless Licensing 1950 to Present* (Rockville, MD, 2000).

[54] U.S. Department of Commerce, *Changes, Challenges, and Charting New Courses: Minority Commercial Broadcast Ownership in the United States* (Washington, D.C., 2000)

[55] FCC has recommended the adoption of a tax deferral program to replace the former tax certificate program that would focus on socially and economically disadvantaged businesses and extend the program to telecommunications.

[56] Seven of 16 case study markets had more than one daily newspaper. However, this ratio is indicative of the selection process for our case study markets in which we selected the three largest DMAs (New York, Los Angeles, and Chicago),which each had more than one daily newspaper, as well as Tucson, which had a joint operating agreement between two daily newspapers. In markets with more than one daily newspaper, we did not evaluate circulation share.

[57] Case study markets with operating agreements were Nashville (1), Wilkes Barre/Scranton (4), Springfield (2), Myrtle Beach/Florence (1), and Terre Haute (1). We also identified two operating agreements for radio stations in Nashville and Harrisonburg.

Appendix I

[1] In smaller urban areas, we defined "close listening distance" as a station which was located within 20 miles of the city or a station located in the Arbitron radio market whose signal contour band covered the urban area. For very large cities, such as Miami, Los Angeles, Chicago, and New York, we used just the signal contour band coverage criteria.

[2] These towns and counties are Sherman, Grayson County, Texas; Ada, Pontotoc County, Oklahoma; Ardmore, Carter County, Oklahoma; and Durant, Bryan County, Oklahoma.

[3] An Arbitron radio market is a geographically contiguous area in which the listnership of radio stations is surveyed for ratings.

[4] *National Ethnic Media Directory*, online version (San Francisco, California: New America Media, Pacific News Service, 2007).

[5] http://news.newamericamedia.org/news/view_custom.html?custom_page_id=263 (downloaded Sept. 28, 2007, through Nov. 6, 2007).

Appendix II

[1] When we refer to "disposable" income, we mean effective buying income, and our source for this information is the Television Bureau of Advertising. The household average effective buying income is a bulk measurement of market potential that indicates the ability to buy and is essential for selecting, comparing, and grouping markets.

[2] That is, a single owner within this particular market only. Most of the commercial radio station owners in the New York City DMA also own numerous stations elsewhere in the United States.

[3] Bear Stearns & Co. Inc., *Bear Stearns Radio Fact Book 2006* (New York, NY, 2006), p. 137.

[4] The eight primary commercial English-language broadcast television networks are ABC, CBS, CW, FOX, ION, MMT, NBC, and TBN.

[5] Determining the number of radio stations in this DMA was difficult because the DMA is small (too small for Arbitron to rate stations within it), yet it is close enough to core urban areas in surrounding DMAs, including the Oklahoma City, Tulsa, and Dallas/Fort Worth markets, to receive signals from stations that are physically located in these markets. We identified the four most populous counties in the Sherman/Ada DMA and selected the largest town within each of these four counties—Sherman, Grayson County, Texas; Ada,

Pontotoc County, Oklahoma; Ardmore, Carter County, Oklahoma; and Durant, Bryan County, Oklahoma. Then we counted all radio stations within 20 miles of each town and checked the list against an atlas to make sure the station was physically located in a county within this DMA.

In: Media Ownership
Editor: Harold F. Velliotis, pp. 67-95
ISBN 978-1-60692-365-8

Chapter 2

THE FCC'S BROADCAST MEDIA OWNERSHIP RULES*

Charles B. Goldfarb

ABSTRACT

The Federal Communications Commission's (FCC or Commission) broadcast media ownership rules are intended to foster the three long-standing goals of U.S. media policy — competition, localism, and diversity of voices. The FCC has the statutory obligation to review these rules every four years to determine if they continue to serve the public interest or should be modified or eliminated. In December 2007, the FCC adopted an order that modified only one of its broadcast media ownership rules — the newspaper-broadcast cross-ownership rule — and left the other rules intact.

Under the new rule, it would be presumptively "not inconsistent with" the public interest, in the 20 largest local markets, for an entity to own both a major daily newspaper and a single television or radio station, so long as the television station is not among the four highest-rated stations in the market and after the transaction there are at least eight independently owned and operating major media voices. Otherwise, in most situations newspaper-broadcast cross-ownership in a local market would be presumptively inconsistent with the public interest. Each proposed combination, however, would be reviewed on a case-by-case basis, and proposed combinations in

---

* Excerpted from CRS Report RL34416, dated May 16, 2008.

smaller markets could be approved. Fifteen parties have appealed the new rule; the challenges will be heard by the United States Court of Appeals for the Ninth Circuit. A joint resolution of disapproval (S.J.Res. 28) to revoke the new rule was approved on a voice vote of the Senate on May 15, 2008, and a similar resolution has been introduced in the House (H.J.Res. 79). In addition, S. 2332 and H.R. 4835 would negate the rule because they would require the FCC, before adopting any new broadcast ownership rule after October 1, 2007, to give 90 days' notice for public comment, which was not done prior to adoption of the rule. In contrast, H.R. 4167 would eliminate the newspaper-radio (but not newspaper-television) cross-ownership prohibition in its entirety.

In its previous quadrennial review, in June 2003, the FCC modified five of its broadcast media ownership rules, easing restrictions on the ownership of multiple television stations (nationally and in local markets) and on local media cross- ownership, and tightening restrictions on the ownership of multiple radio stations in local markets. Those rules have never gone into effect. Sec. 629 of the FY2004 Consolidated Appropriations Act (P.L. 108-199) instructed the FCC to modify its new National Television Ownership rule to allow a broadcast network to own and operate local broadcast stations that reach, in total, at most 39% of U.S. television households. In June 2004, the United States Court of Appeal for the Third Circuit, in *Prometheus Radio Project vs. Federal Communications Commission,* found that the FCC did not provide reasoned analysis to support its specific local ownership limits, and also that the FCC failed to address the impact of it new rules on minority ownership of broadcast stations, and therefore remanded portions of the new local ownership rules back to the FCC and extended its stay of those rules.

CURRENT STATUS [1]

The Federal Communications Commission's (FCC or Commission) broadcast media ownership rules are intended to foster the three long-standing goals of U.S. media policy — competition, localism, and diversity of voices. The FCC is required by statute to review these rules every four years to determine if they continue to serve the public interest or should be modified or eliminated. [2] In addition, in 2004 the FCC was instructed by the United States Court of Appeals for the Third Circuit (Third Circuit) "to justify or modify" the broadcast local ownership rules that it had adopted in 2003 as part of its statutory periodic review. [3] The Third Circuit found that the Commission had not provided reasoned analysis to support the specific ownership limits in those rules:

> The Commission's derivation of new Cross-Media Limits, and its modification of the numerical limits on both television and radio station ownership in local markets, all have the same essential flaw: an unjustified assumption that media outlets of the same type make an equal contribution to diversity and competition in local markets. We thus remand for the Commission to justify or modify its approach to setting numerical limits. [4]

As a result of the Third Circuit's stay and remand of the broadcast local ownership rules that the FCC had adopted in 2003,5 the broadcast media ownership rules that had been in place prior to the FCC's adoption of its Order on June 2, 2003 were reinstated — except that in the interim Congress passed Section 629 of the FY2004 Consolidated Appropriations Act (P.L. 108-199), which instructed the FCC to modify its National Television Ownership rule.

Responding to these statutory and judicial instructions, in December 2007 the FCC adopted an order that modified its newspaper-broadcast cross-ownership rule, but left its other broadcast local ownership rules intact. [6] Two commissioners dissented from the order. [7]

Given these congressional, regulatory, and judicial actions, the current status of the FCC's broadcast media ownership rules is as follows.

Newspaper-Broadcast Cross-Ownership

The specifics of the newly adopted rule. On December 18, 2007, the FCC adopted an order that modified the newspaper-broadcast cross-ownership rule. [8] The new rule, which cannot go into effect until it has been approved by the courts, [9] would replace the current rule that prohibits cross-ownership of a newspaper and a television or radio station in a local market. A number of such combinations currently exist, however, because when the FCC first adopted the cross-ownership prohibition in 1975 it grandfathered some pre-existing combinations and, in the past few years, the FCC has granted a number of newspaper-broadcast combinations temporary waivers, pending conclusion of its quadrennial review proceeding. In its 2007 Order, the FCC granted permanent waivers to five of those newspaper- broadcast station combinations [10].

The new newspaper-broadcast cross-ownership rule is complex. Every proposed newspaper-broadcast combination in which the signal of the broadcast station encompasses the entire community in which the newspaper is published is subject to a public interest determination with three distinct steps. [11]

First, the new rule establishes a bright line test, with strict numerical limits, to identify proposed combinations that would be deemed presumptively "not inconsistent with the public interest." [12] Specifically, it would be presumptively not inconsistent with the public interest for an entity to own both a major daily newspaper and a single television or radio station in a single local market if:

- the combination is in one of the 20 largest local markets; [13] and,
- if the broadcast station is a television station, the station is not among the four highest-rated stations in the market; and,
- after the transaction there still are at least eight independently owned and operating major media voices in the market. [14]

These three bright line numerical limits are straight-forward and easy to objectively identify.

All other proposed newspaper-broadcast station combinations in a local market would be deemed presumptively inconsistent with the public interest. [15]

Second, the new rule specifies two circumstances that, if met, would automatically reverse a negative presumption about a proposed combination. [16] Specifically, the negative presumption would be automatically reversed if either:

- the newspaper or broadcast station has failed or is failing; [17] or
- the proposed combination is with a broadcast station that was not offering local newscasts prior to the combination, and the station would initiate at least seven hours per week of local news programming after the combination. [18]

These circumstances are relatively straight-forward and relatively easy to objectively identify. Although the second circumstance cannot be demonstrated in advance of the combination, the 2007 Order states that "broadcast station licenses that are approved as a result of this reversal presumption will need to report to the Commission annually regarding how they have followed through on their commitment to initiate at least seven hours a week of local news." [19] The 2007 Order does not identify, however, a process to use if the commitment is not met.

Third, the new rule identifies four factors that would be considered to confirm or rebut the positive or negative public interest presumption about a proposed combination, to yield a final public interest determination. [20] Specifically, for any proposed newspaper-broadcast station combination in a local market — whether it met the criteria for a positive or negative public interest presumption —

the FCC would be required to make a public interest determination considering the following four factors:

- whether the combined entity will significantly increase the amount of local news in the market; [21]
- whether the newspaper and the broadcast outlets each will continue to employ its own staff and each will exercise its own independent news judgment;
- the level of concentration in the DMA; and
- the financial condition of the newspaper or broadcast station, and if the newspaper or broadcast is in financial distress, the proposed owner's commitment to invest significantly in newsroom operations.

Where this public interest determination is being made for a proposed combination that has a negative presumption, "the applicant must show by clear and convincing evidence that the co-owned major newspaper and station will increase the diversity of independent news outlets and increase competition among independent news sources in the market," with the four factors listed above informing this decision." [22]

The discussion in the 2007 Order identifies these as factors to be used to rebut a negative presumption, [23] but does not indicate whether the FCC may consider additional factors or what weight, if any, it should give these four factors in making its public interest determination. These four factors are not always easy to objectively identify or measure; three involve commitments on the part of the applicant to future actions. Neither the rule nor the language in the 2007 Order address what recourse the FCC or affected parties would have if the applicant did not live up to its commitments once it obtained the license.

Given the mandatory public interest determination in the adopted rule, a proposed newspaper-broadcast combination in a top-20 market, with eight or more independent major media voices, and not involving a top-four television station, although not presumptively inconsistent with the public interest, could nonetheless be rejected by the Commission. Similarly, a proposed newspaper-broadcast combination in a non-top-20 market, or in a market with fewer than eight independent major media voices, or involving a top-four television station, and thus presumptively inconsistent with the public interest, could nonetheless be approved by the Commission.

On one hand, the complexity of the new rule potentially allows for a detailed, sophisticated analysis of the public interest implications of a proposed newspaper-broadcast station combination. On the other hand, its complexity, and the reliance on commitments to future behavior and subjective factors, potentially allows a majority of the Commission to justify whatever determination it reaches.

In its order adopting the new rule, the Commission stated:

> To the extent that a proposed combination does not qualify for a positive presumption, it will have a high hurdle to cross to win Commission approval. [24]

But in that same order, the Commission granted permanent waivers to five newspaper-broadcast combinations [25] although the combinations did not appear to meet all the criteria to be presumptively in the public interest. The brief discussion (comprised of a single paragraph plus footnotes) addressing these permanent waivers did not provide the sort of detailed case-by-case analysis that some might expect to be required to cross "a high hurdle." Citing these waivers, the two FCC commissioners who had dissented from the 2007 Order issued a strongly worded statement questioning whether the new rule would be interpreted in a fashion that would create "loopholes" that would allow many cross-ownership combinations that are not presumptively in the public interest, rather than constituting a high hurdle to limit such combinations. [26]

The FCC's justification of the numerical limits in the rule. Since the Third Circuit found that the FCC had failed to justify the numerical limits in the rules it had adopted in 2003, and the new FCC rule incorporates a number of numerical limits in both its positive and negative public interest presumptions, the 2007 Order discussed the record evidence underlying each of the numerical elements in its new newspaper-broadcast cross-ownership rule. [27]

- The FCC limited the presumption that a newspaper-broadcast combination would be in the public interest to the top 20 DMAs because there was evidence in the record showing differences between the top 20 DMAs and all other DMAs, in terms of the number of independent voices. The data showed that while there are at least 10 independently owned television stations in 18 of the top 20 DMAs, none of the DMAs ranked 21 through 25 have 10 independently owned television stations; while 17 of the top 20 DMAs have at least two newspapers with a circulation of at least 5% of the households in that DMA, four of the five DMAs ranked 21 through 25 have only one such newspaper. [28]
- The FCC limited the presumption that a newspaper-broadcast combination would be in the public interest to markets in which there still would be eight independent major media voices after the combination

because it found that these major media voices are generally the most important and relevant outlets for news and information in local markets today. [29] It justified basing its presumption on the number of major media voices — rather than all media voices — by citing relatively unanimous support in the record for the position that consumers continue predominantly to get their local news from daily newspapers and broadcast television. Data on the record show that consumers rely mostly on newspapers and television for news and information. Other media outlets contribute to diversity, but those other voices are not major sources of local news or information, and thus they are not included in the definition of major media voices. [30] The FCC did not provide empirical justification for the bright line numerical limit of eight independent major media voices, however. It "selected the number eight for the major media voice count because we are comfortable that assuring that minimum number of major media voices in the top 20 markets — along with the other unquantified media outlets that are present in those markets — will assure that these markets continue to enjoy an adequate diversity of local news and information sources." [31] It noted that all the top 20 markets have at least eight television stations and one major newspaper, and stated that it did "not want to allow a significant decrease in the number of independently owned major media voices in any of those markets" and thus imposed the requirement that there be at least eight major media voices post- combination.

- The FCC limited the presumption that a newspaper-television combination in the top 20 DMAs would be in the public interest to those situations in which the television station is not one of the top four rated stations in the market because it considered a daily newspaper and the top four stations to be the most influential providers of local news in their market; thus the combination of a newspaper with a top four station is likely to cause greater harm to diversity in the market than other combinations. [32] Moreover, the FCC believed "that combinations of newspapers and non-top four television stations are more likely to result in the production of more local news in furtherance of our localism goal." [33] According to the FCC, the available data show that stations below the top four are less likely to carry local news, and therefore more likely to carry "new news" as a result of a newspaper combination; specifically, 86% of stations ranked first through fourth in all DMAs provide local news, averaging 2083 minutes, while only 40% of stations ranked fifth and below in all DMAs provide some local news, averaging 458 minutes.

[34] While the top-four station numerical limit has intuitive appeal since it conforms with the four major national broadcast television networks (ABC, CBS, Fox, and NBC), [35] it is not clear that the cited data are relevant to a determination that the proper limit is the top four stations. The FCC compares averages for the top four stations to averages for all remaining stations, and finds sharp differences. But these averages provide no information about whether there is a significant change in the amount of local news provided by the fourth and fifth stations in a market. Moreover, the data presented are for all DMAs, but the presumption is limited to the top 20 markets. The Commission does not indicate whether the sharp difference in averages between the top four stations and all additional stations that holds when looking at all DMAs also holds when looking only at the top 20 markets.

- The FCC would reverse a negative presumption toward a proposed newspaper/broadcast combination if the broadcast outlet has not been offering local newscasts prior to the combination, but would initiate local news programming of at least seven hours per week as a result of the combination, because "the Commission has historically considered [broadcasters'] news and public affairs programming to be uniquely and particularly important," and thus a "positive presumption under this limited circumstance will increase diversity of choices, provide more local programming, and allow better local service by media outlets." [36] In the discussion of this criterion for reversing a negative presumption, the Order provides no explanation for how the Commission selected the seven hour numerical limit. But in the discussion of factors to be used to rebut a presumption, the Order states, without explanation, "we consider a significant increase to be at least seven hours a week of additional news in the market." [37] The discussion in the Order does not address whether this criterion might create a perverse incentive. Yet an existing station seeking to be purchased might expect that a local newspaper would value that station more highly than other potential purchasers from outside the market, and thus might have the incentive to discontinue offering local news programming in order to allow its purchase by that newspaper under the "initiates local news programming" criterion.
- • One of the four factors to be considered when confirming or rebutting a public interest presumption about a proposed combination is "whether the combined entity will significantly increase the amount of local news in the market." [38] Interestingly, it is in its discussion of this factor that the Commission references seven hours of programming per week as a

significant increase, but in the rule, itself, there is no mention of seven hours or any measure of a significant increase. [39] Moreover, it appears that this factor would only consider the impact of the proposed combination on the amount of local news programming offered by the combining newspaper and broadcast station. It would not consider the impact of the proposed combination on total local news programming in the local market. It is possible, however, that the combined newspaper-broadcast entity could command advertising revenues and audience share to the detriment of the other broadcasters in the market, and that as a result those other broadcasters might reduce or eliminate their local news programming, which sometimes is expensive to produce. The comments submitted in the record by a group of consumer organizations [40] included econometric studies that purportedly show that newspaper-broadcast cross-ownership decreases the total amount of local news provided in a market. In its 2007 Order, however, the FCC found "numerous difficulties" with that analysis, however, and concluded that it "cannot rely on its conclusions." [41] Nonetheless, it is not clear why the FCC would not consider the impact of a proposed combination on the amount of market-wide local news programming in its public interest determination.

Challenges to the new rule. The new newspaper-broadcast cross- ownership rule has been appealed both by parties opposing any loosening of the FCC's newspaper-broadcast cross-ownership rule and parties seeking greater loosening of the rule. [42] As indicated earlier, the new rule has been appealed by 15 parties and the Ninth Circuit was chosen at random to hear the challenges. It is likely that an affected party that favors the rule change will petition the court to end the current stay and allow the rule to go in effect pending court review.

In December 2007, just before the FCC voted to adopt the new rule, a bipartisan group of 25 senators informed the FCC of its intention to pass a joint resolution of disapproval to revoke the rule. [43] A joint resolution of disapproval cannot be introduced until the rule has been published in the Federal Register and transmitted to Congress, however. [44] On March 5, 2008, once the new rule had been transmitted to Congress, Senator Dorgan introduced S.J.Res. 28, a resolution of disapproval to block the new rule. [45] On March 13, 2008, Representative Inslee introduced a companion House resolution (H.J.Res. 79). In early April 2008, the President's advisers said they would recommend a veto of the resolution should it reach the President's desk. [46] On May 15, 2008, the Senate approved S.J.Res. 28 on a voice vote. The White House reiterated its intention to veto the joint resolution. [47] Also, S. 2332 (introduced by Senator Dorgan) and H.R. 4835 (introduced by Representative Inslee) would negate the rule because they would require the FCC, before adopting any new broadcast ownership rule after October 1, 2007, to give 90 days' notice for public comment, which was not done prior to adoption of the rule. [48] In contrast, H.R. 4167 (introduced by Representative Stearns) would eliminate the newspaper-broadcast radio (but not television) cross-ownership prohibition in its entirety.

Television-Radio Cross-Ownership

In its 2003 Order, the FCC adopted a new, less restrictive Television-Radio Cross-Ownership rule, but the Third Circuit remanded that rule and extended its stay that left in place the rule that the FCC had adopted in 1999. That rule remains in place today. Under the rule:

- An entity may own up to two television stations (provided it is permitted under the Local Television Multiple Ownership rule) and up to six radio stations (provided it is permitted under the Local Radio Multiple Ownership rule) in a market where at least 20 independently owned media voices would remain post-merger.
- Where entities may own a combination of two television stations and six radio stations, the rule allows an entity alternatively to own one television station and seven radio stations.
- An entity may own up to two television stations (as permitted under the Local Television Multiple Ownership rule) and up to four radio stations (as permitted under the Local Radio Multiple Ownership rule) in markets where, post-merger, at least 10 independently owned media voices would remain.
- A combination of one television station and one radio station is allowed regardless of the number of voices remaining in the market. [49]

In its 2007 Order, the FCC retained the existing Television-Radio Multiple-Ownership rule, concluding that, in the absence of the cross-media limits that it had adopted in 2003 but that the Third Circuit had remanded, the existing rule provided protection for diversity goals in local markets and thereby served the public interest. [50] Citing its 1999 Order creating the current rule, the Commission found that "Because the two media 'serve as substitutes at least to some degree for diversity purposes,' there remains a need to retain a cross-ownership rule 'to ensure that viewpoint diversity is adequately protected.'" [51] The Commission did not find support in the record for either tightening or loosening the current rule. [52]

Local Television Multiple Ownership

In its 2003 Order, the FCC adopted a new, less restrictive Local Television Multiple Ownership rule, but the Third Circuit remanded that rule and extended its stay that left in place the rule that the FCC had adopted in 1999, which is sometimes referred to as the "TV duopoly" rule. Under this rule, an entity may own two television stations in the same DMA only if the following requirements are met:

- either the Grade B contours [53] of the stations do not overlap, or
- at least one of the stations is not ranked among the four highest- ranked stations in the DMA, and (b) at least eight independently owned and operating commercial or non-commercial full-power broadcast television stations would remain in the DMA after the proposed combination were consummated. [54]

This second option is sometimes referred to as the "top four ranked/eight voices test." An existing licensee of a failed, failing, or unbuilt television station may seek a waiver of the rule. [55] Any combination formed as a result of a failed, failing, or unbuilt station waiver may be transferred together only if the combination meets the Local Television Multiple Ownership rule or one of the three waiver standards at the time of transfer. [56]

In its 2007 Order, the FCC found that:

> in order to preserve adequate levels of competition within local television markets, the local television ownership rule as it is currently in effect should be retained. [57]

This finding reverses the finding in its 2003 Order that the existing rule was not necessary to protect competition. [58] The Commission also reversed the finding in its 2003 Order that the current rule potentially threatens local programming and that the efficiencies to be gained by relaxing the rule could result in a higher quantity and quality of local news and public affairs programming, finding that the evidentiary record is unpersuasive regarding the effects of multiple ownership on local programming [59]. In its 2007 Order, the FCC reinstated the requirement that the applicant demonstrate that the "in-market" buyer was the only reasonably available entity willing and able to operate the subject station, which it had previously repealed. [60].

In its Prometheus decision, the Third Circuit had remanded the repeal of that requirement because the Commission had failed to address the original purpose of the requirement — to ensure that qualified minority broadcasters had a fair chance to learn that certain financially troubled, and consequently more affordable, stations were for sale. [61]

Local Radio Multiple Ownership

The ownership limits currently in place are those that the FCC adopted in 1996 to codify the language in Section 202(b)(1) of the 1996 Telecommunications Act, but, as a result of the Third Circuit agreeing in rehearing to lift the portion of its stay relating to the FCC's new methodology for defining local radio markets, those markets are defined using that new methodology. Specifically, the current rules provide that:

- in a radio market with 45 or more full power commercial and noncommercial radio stations, an entity may own, operate, or control up to eight commercial radio stations, not more than five of which are in the same service (AM or FM);
- in a radio market with between 30 and 44 (inclusive) full power commercial and noncommercial radio stations, an entity may own, operate, or control up to seven commercial radio stations, not more than four of which are in the same service (AM or FM);
- in a radio market with between 15 and 29 (inclusive) full power commercial and noncommercial radio stations, an entity may own, operate, or control up to six commercial radio stations, not more than four of which are in the same service (AM or FM);
- in a radio market with 14 or fewer full power commercial and noncommercial radio stations, an entity may own, operate, or control up to five commercial radio stations, not more than three of which are in the same service (AM or FM), except that an entity may not own, operate, or control more than 50 percent of the stations in such market. [62]

These numerical limits are applied to geographic markets that are defined according to Arbitron rating boundaries, which are based on market factors rather than on the signal transmission contours that previously were used to define markets [63].

Since Arbitron boundaries do not cover small radio markets, the FCC performed a rulemaking proceeding to determine how to define geographic markets in those small markets for which there are no Arbitron market definitions. [64]. Also, under current rules, when a "brokering" station has a Joint Sales Agreement (JSA) with a "brokered" station — typically this authorizes one station acting as a broker to sell advertising time for the brokered station in return for a fee — the brokered stations counts toward the number of stations the brokering licensee may own in a local market. [65]

In its 2007 Order, the FCC concluded that all the specific elements in the current Local Radio Ownership rule — including the specific ownership tiers, numerical limits, and AM/FM subcaps, as well as the market definitions revised in 2003 — remain "necessary in the public interest" to protection competition in local radio markets, [66] although it employs a different rationale for justifying these limits than it used in its 2003 Order. In the 2007 Order, it found that

> By maintaining the current numerical limits, we seek to guard against additional consolidation of the strongest stations in a market in the hands of too few owners and to ensure a market structure that fosters opportunities for new entry into radio broadcasting. The number of commercial radio station owners declined by 39 percent between 1996 and 2007, with most of the decline occurring during the first few years after the 1996 Act. Although the average number of commercial owners across all Arbitron radio markets currently is 9.4, the largest commercial firm in each Arbitron Metro market has, on average, 46 percent of the market's total radio advertising revenue, and the largest two firms have 74 percent of the revenue. In 111 of the 299 Arbitron Metro markets, the top two commercial station owners control at least 80 percent of radio advertising revenue. The top four commercial firms also dominate audience share. And evidence in the record indicates that the increase in concentration in commercial radio markets has resulted in appreciable, albeit small, increases in advertising rates. All of this data in the record supports the conclusion that the current numerical limits are not unduly restrictive and that additional consolidation would not serve the Commission's competitive goals. (Footnotes omitted.) [67]

The Commission also found:

> By preserving a healthy, competitive local radio market, the local radio ownership rule helps promote our interest in localism. Aside from the positive

> effect on localism that ensues from a competitive radio market, however, the Commission has never found that the local radio ownership rule significantly advances our interest in localism. [68]

Similarly, based on its examination of the record, the Commission

> cannot conclude that the local radio ownership rule is necessary to protect format diversity. Nevertheless, we find that retaining the current, competition-based numerical limits on local radio ownership will promote diversity indirectly.... Thus, it is proper for us to retain the status quo, as the ownership tiers serve the public interest in light of competition. [69]

In the 2007 Order, the Commission also found that retaining the current, competition- based AM/FM subcaps "will promote diversity indirectly by facilitating and encouraging entry into the local media market by new and underrepresented parties, and we thus conclude that the AM subcaps are in the public interest." [70]

National Television Ownership (% Cap)

A broadcast network may own and operate local broadcast stations that reach, in total, up to 39% of U.S. television households; entities that exceed the 39% cap must divest as needed to come into compliance within two years; the FCC may not forbear on applying the 39% cap; and the FCC is prohibited from performing the quadrennial review of the 39% cap. [71]

In practice, the National Television Ownership rule applies to the major broadcast networks, limiting them to ownership and operation of local broadcast stations that reach, in total, the prescribed percentage of U.S. television households. When calculating the total audience reached by an entity's stations, the so- called "UHF discount" is applied — audiences of UHF stations are given only halfweight. [72]

For example, if an entity owns a UHF station in a market with an audience of two million households, that audience would only be counted as one million households when calculating the entity's market reach. In its 2007 Order, the FCC found that

> the Commission is foreclosed from addressing the issue of the UHF discount in this proceeding by the 2004 Consolidated Appropriations Act. Although the Act did not specifically mention the UHF discount, the Prometheus court

> observed that the statutory 39 percent national cap would be altered if the UHF discount were modified.... Accordingly, we conclude that the UHF discount is insulated from review under Section 202(h). [73]

However, the Commission noted that the Third Circuit recognized that the FCC might have authority, outside Section 202(h) to modify or eliminate the UHF discount, and that the FCC had sought public comment on the scope of that authority prior to the Third Circuit's Prometheus decision. [74] The Commission therefore decided to separately address the extent of its authority to alter the UHF discount and whether it should retain, revise, or eliminate the discount.

Dual Network Ownership

The Dual Network Ownership rule permits common ownership of multiple broadcast networks, but prohibits a merger among the "top four" networks — ABC, CBS, Fox, and NBC. [75] In both its 2003 Order and its 2007 Order, the FCC retained the rule [76].

In both reviews, the Commission found that the rule continues to be necessary to promote competition in the national television advertising and program acquisition markets, and that the rule promotes localism by preserving the balance of negotiating power between networks and affiliates.

In 2001, as part of an earlier biennial review of its broadcast media ownership rules, the FCC had modified this rule to allow the four major networks to own, operate, maintain, or control broadcast networks other than the four majors. With this change, Viacom, the owner of CBS, was allowed to purchase UPN, and NBC was able to purchase Telemundo, the second largest Spanish-language network in the United States.

Impact of the Broadcast Media Ownership Rules on Minority Ownership

In its Prometheus decision, the Third Circuit also found that the FCC had failed to address the impact of its new rules on minority ownership of broadcast stations and instructed the Commission to address in its rulemaking process proposals for advancing minority and disadvantaged businesses and for promoting diversity in broadcasting that the Minority Media Telecommunications Council (MMTC) had submitted in the proceeding in 2003. [77]

Responding to this court instruction, in December 2007 the FCC adopted an order that implemented 12 of the 34 proposals to foster minority ownership of broadcast stations that the Commission had put out for comment in an August 1, 2007, Second Further Notice of Proposed Rulemaking. [78] Eligibility for these programs was not limited, however, to minority or socially and economically disadvantaged businesses, but rather was available to all small businesses. [79] A companion Notice of Proposed Rulemaking sought comment on eligibility criteria and on how best to improve FCC collection of data regarding the gender, race, and ethnicity of broadcast licensees.

Underlying Issues: Standard of Review, Bright Line Tests, Case-by-Case Evaluations, and Waivers

The FCC has the statutory obligation to perform a quadrennial review of its broadcast media ownership rules. In performing this review, the Commission must address several fundamental issues that have potentially significant policy implications.

First, what is the relevant standard for reaching a public interest determination about existing ownership rules?

Second, what are the advantages and disadvantages of using bright line tests vs. case-by-case evaluations when making a public interest determination about a proposed ownership transactions that would increase media concentration? Is there a distinction between the two approaches when there is a waiver process available to parties that do not meet a bright line test?

Standard of Review

There has been some controversy surrounding the standard to be used in reaching a public interest determination about the existing rules. The D.C. Circuit, in Fox Television Stations, Inc. v. Federal Communications Commission, stated "Section 202(h) carries with it a presumption in favor of repealing or modifying the ownership rules." [80] Further, in response to petitions for rehearing, the D.C. Circuit stated "[T]he statute is clear that a regulation should be retained only insofar as it is necessary in, not merely consonant with, the public interest." [81] But in the same decision, the D.C. Circuit stated that "[t]he Court's decision did not turn at all upon interpreting 'necessary in the public interest' to mean more than 'in the public interest'" and added "we think it better to leave unresolved precisely what § 202(h) means when it instructs the Commission first to determine whether a rule is 'necessary in the public interest' but then to 'repeal or modify' the rule if it is simply 'no longer in the public interest.'" [82]

In its 2003 Order, the FCC majority took this language to mean that the Commission must overcome a high burden to retain any ownership rule. Responding to a question from Senator McCain in a June 4, 2003 Senate Commerce Committee hearing, then-FCC chairman Powell stated that the D.C. Circuit interprets the act to be "biased toward deregulation" and added that for the Commission to be in concert with that interpretation it "cannot re-regulate." In response to a question from Senator Dorgan, then-FCC commissioner Abernathy stated that the D.C. Circuit's interpretation directs the Commission to minimize regulation as competition develops, not to regulate to maximize the number of voices.

At that same hearing, all five FCC commissioners and several Senators agreed that it would be useful for Congress to provide both the Court and the Commission guidance on the standard to use for reviewing ownership rules and on whether the act allows the commission to re-regulate broadcast ownership.

Subsequently, in its Prometheus decision, the Third Circuit found:

> While we acknowledge that § 202(h) was enacted in the context of deregulatory amendments (the 1996 Act) to the Communications Act, see Fox I, 280 F.3d at 1033; Sinclair, 284 F.3d at 159, we do not accept that the "repeal or modify in the public interest" instruction must therefore operate only as a one-way ratchet, i.e., the Commission can use the review process only to eliminate then-extant regulations. For starters, this ignores both "modify" and the requirement that the Commission act "in the public interest." ...
>
> Rather than "upending" the reasoned analysis requirement that under the APA ordinarily applies to an agency's decision to promulgate new regulations (or modify or repeal existing regulations), see State Farm, 463 U.S. at 43, § 202(h) extends this requirement to the Commission's decision to retain its existing regulations. This interpretation avoids a crabbed reading of the statute under which we would have to infer, without express language, that Congress intended to curtail the Commission's rulemaking authority to contravene "traditional administrative law principles." [83]

Bright Line Tests, Case-by-Case Evaluations, and Waivers

In its 2003 Order, the FCC reviewed the advantages and disadvantages of implementing bright line rules that incorporate specific limits on the number of media outlets a company can own in a local market (without regard to such market- specific characteristics as the market share of the post-merger company or the degree to which the merging company is vertically integrated into program production) vs. implementing flexible, yet quantifiable rules that would allow for case-by-case reviews that more readily take into account market-specific or company-specific market shares and characteristics.

The Commission chose the bright line approach, in large part because it identified regulatory certainty as an important policy goal in addition to the three traditional goals of diversity, competition, and localism. [84] The Commission stated:

> Any benefit to precision of a case-by-case review is outweighed, in our view, by the harm caused by a lack of regulatory certainty to the affected firms and to the capital markets that fund the growth and innovation in the media industry. Companies seeking to enter or exit the media market or seeking to grow larger or smaller will all benefit from clear rules in making business plans and investment decisions. Clear structural rules permit planning of financial transactions, ease application processing, and minimize regulatory costs. [85]

It concluded that the adoption of bright line rules rather than case-by-case analysis provides certainty to outcomes, conserves resources, reduces administrative delays, lowers transactions costs, increases transparency of process, and ensures consistency in decisions, all of which foster capital investment in broadcasting. The Commission conceded that bright line rules preclude a certain amount of flexibility.

The 2003 Order did not explain how the Commission would weigh the goal of regulatory certainty vis-à-vis the traditional goals of diversity, competition, and localism, if the former were to be in conflict with one or more of the latter. On one hand, the Commission stated that it would continue to have discretion to review particular cases, and would have an obligation to take a hard look both at waiver requests (where a bright line ownership limit would proscribe a particular transaction) and at petitions to deny a license transfer (where a bright line ownership limit would allow a particular transaction). At the same time, however, it suggested it would not look favorably upon some petitions:

> Bright lines provide the certainty and predictability needed for companies to make business plans and for capital markets to make investments in the growth and innovation in media markets. Conversely, case-by-case review of even below-cap mergers on diversity grounds would lead to uncertainty and undermine our efforts to encourage growth in broadcast services. Accordingly, petitioners should not use the petition to deny process to relitigate the issues resolved in this proceeding. [86]

Having determined that a bright line test was preferable to case-by-case review, the Commission created bright line tests for its broadcast media cross-ownership and local ownership rules. The Third Circuit found that the Commission's decision to retain a bright line numerical limits approach to broadcast ownership rules was "rational and in the public interest," [87] but found the methodology used by the Commission to set those numerical limits arbitrary.

In its 2007 Order, the FCC has changed direction, opting for a rule that incorporates elements of both a bright line approach (presumptions with specific numerical limits) and a case-by-case approach (factors that the Commission would consider in the case-by-case review of both combinations that met the presumption of being in the public interest and combinations that did not). The FCC was motivated in part by the fact that elements of the evidentiary record were inconclusive and therefore not supportive of strict bright line numerical limits. The Commission found:

> The inconclusiveness of some of the data and disagreement as to the outcome of the studies, however, supports our decision to undertake a case-by-case review of particular combinations in particular markets, rather than providing hard, across-the-board limits. Under our method, we can consider facts in a particular case, with a presumption in favor of allowing newspaper and radio station or non-top four television station combinations in the top 20 markets, and a presumption against combinations in all other markets. A case-by-case approach will enable the Commission to make a more fully informed assessment that a proposed transaction in a particular market actually will increase the total amount of local news generated by the combined outlets. [88]
>
> Establishing presumptions, as opposed to a bright line, will allow for the evaluation of proposed newspaper/broadcast combinations under defined circumstances on a case-by-case basis. [89]

At the same time, the FCC concluded in its 2007 Order that, based on the evidentiary record in the proceeding, it was appropriate to maintain the current numerical limits in its other broadcast ownership rules. [90] In that Order, however, the Commission did not present data to support all the specific numerical limits in those rules.

Thus, currently, most of the broadcast media ownership rules have bright line numerical limits, but the newspaper-broadcast cross-ownership rule is more flexible, requiring the FCC to make a case-by-case public interest evaluation.

There may not be a sharp distinction, however, between rules with bright line numerical limits and rules requiring case-by-case evaluations because parties may seek waivers of bright-line rules and, to the extent the FCC grants such waivers, the effect may be to provide equal or even greater flexibility. This is particularly apparent in recent FCC waiver decisions involving newspaper-broadcast station combinations in local markets.

When the FCC adopted its new newspaper-broadcast cross-ownership rule, in the same Order it granted permanent waivers to five newspaper-broadcast combinations. [91] As explained earlier, the combinations that were granted waivers did not appear to meet all the criteria in the new rule to be presumptively in the public interest and the brief discussion addressing these permanent waivers did not provide the sort of detailed case-by-case analysis that would appear to be required under the new rule.

These waiver grants followed closely upon controversial waiver grants made by the Commission in November 2007. At that time, the FCC issued a Memorandum Opinion and Order, with commissioners Copps and Adelstein dissenting, [92] granting the applications to transfer control of Tribune Company and its licensee subsidiaries from the existing shareholders to Sam Zell, the Tribune Employee Stock Ownership Plan, and EGI-TRB, LLC. The transferees had requested temporary, but indefinite, waiver of the newspaper-broadcast cross-ownership rule to permit common ownership pending the outcome of the Media Ownership proceeding of: KTLA(TV), Los Angeles, and the Los Angeles Times; WPIX(TV), New York, and Newsday; WGN-TV and WGN(AM), Chicago, and the Chicago Tribune; WSFL(TV), Miami, and the Ft. Lauderdale South Florida Sun-Sentinel; and WTIC(TV), Hartford, WTTX(Waterbury), and the Hartford Courier. The FCC denied the requested waivers in all the markets except Chicago, requiring the Transferees to come into compliance with the newspaper-broadcast cross-ownership rule in all the markets except Chicago within six months. However, the order noted that the Commission was scheduled to vote on a revised newspaper-broadcast cross-ownership rule at its December 18, 2007, meeting, and therefore took the following three steps:

- The six-month clock for coming into compliance with the newspaper-broadcast cross-ownership rule in New York, Los Angeles, Miami, and Hartford would not begin running until January 1, 2008.
- Should the FCC adopt a revised newspaper-broadcast cross- ownership rule before January 1, 2008, that six-month clock would not begin to run. Rather, the applicants would receive a two-year waiver of the rule for the New York, Los Angeles, Miami, and Hartford markets.
- Should the applicants choose to challenge the denial of waivers in court, they were granted a temporary waiver of the newspaper- broadcast cross-ownership rule for the New York, Los Angeles, Miami, and Hartford markets that would last either for two years or until six months after the conclusion of the litigation, whichever is longer.

The applicants did file an appeal on December 3, 2007, of the denial of its request for indefinite waivers in the U.S. Court of Appeals court. [93]

In dissenting from the FCC decision, Commissioner Michael Copps stated:

> If the majority simply granted a two-year waiver to Tribune — which would have been the straightforward thing to do — Tribune would have been unable to go to court because a party cannot file an appeal if their waiver request is granted. So what does this Order do? It *denies* the waiver request but offers an automatic (and unprecedented) waiver extension as soon as Tribune runs to the courthouse door, lasting for two years or until the litigation concludes — whichever is *longer*. Presto! Tribune gets at least a two-year waiver plus the ability to go to court immediately and see if they can get the entire rule thrown out. And most important, Tribune is not required to seek a hearing before the very court which expressly retained jurisdiction when it remanded the general newspaper- broadcast cross-ownership ban. Instead, Tribune can end run the Third Circuit and petition for review before what it may hope is a more sympathetic court. (emphasis in original.) [94]

The Tribune waiver and the waivers in the 2007 Order lend at least the appearance that the majority at the FCC used the existing waiver process to approve newspaper-broadcast combinations that might not have met the requirements of either the old or the new cross-ownership rule. This suggests that it may be less important whether the ownership rules have bright lines or require case-by-case evaluations. Both the waiver process for bright line rules and the evaluation process for case-by-case public interest determinations appear to give the FCC commissioners a significant degree of discretion in their decision making and allow them to choose to enforce ownership limits more or less stringently.

References

[1] For a detailed discussion of the historical development of the FCC's broadcast media ownership rules, and especially of FCC actions during the 2003-2007 period, see CRS Report RL31925, *FCC Media Ownership Rules, Current Status and Issues for Congress*, by Charles B. Goldfarb.

[2] Section 629 of the FY2004 Consolidated Appropriations Act, P.L. 108-199, modified Section 202(h) of the Telecommunications Act of 1996 (P.L. 104-104), instructing the FCC to perform a quadrennial review of all of its media ownership rules, except the National Television Ownership rule.

[3] *Prometheus Radio Project v. Federal Communications Commission, 373 F.3d 372, 435 (3rd Circuit 2004) (Prometheus).* The decision is available at [http://www.ca3.uscourts.gov/ opinarch/033388p.pdf], viewed on March 6, 2008. For a legal perspective on the Prometheus decision, see CRS Report RL32460, Legal Challenge to the FCC's Media Ownership Rules: An Overview of Prometheus Radio v. FCC, by Kathleen Ann Ruane. Although the Third Circuit remanded the FCC's specific cross-media ownership, local television multiple ownership, and local radio multiple ownership rules, and extended the stay, it upheld many of the FCC's findings, including: not to retain a ban on newspaper- broadcast cross-ownership; to retain some limits on common ownership of different-type media outlets; to retain the restriction on owning more than one top-four television station in a market; the Commission's new definition of local radio markets; to include non-commercial stations in determining the size of local radio markets; the Commission's restriction on the transfer of radio stations; to count radio stations brokered under a Joint Sales Agreement toward the brokering station's permissible ownership totals; and to use numerical limits in its ownership rules (though not the specific numerical limits adopted by the Commission).

[4] The decision went on to state: "The stay currently in effect will continue pending our review of the Commission's action on remand, over which this panel retains jurisdiction." However, when 15 parties filed appeals of the rule in a number of different federal circuit courts of appeal, the United States Court of Appeals for the Ninth Circuit (Ninth Circuit) was chosen at random from among the courts where appeals were filed to hear the challenges. See "Mass Media Notes," *Communications Daily*, March 11, 2008.

[5] The rules adopted by the FCC in its 2003 Order can be found in *In the Matter of 2002 Biennial Regulatory Review — Review of the Commission's*

Broadcast Ownership Rules and Other Rules Adopted Pursuant to Section 202 of the Telecommunications Act of 1996; Cross-Ownership of Broadcast Stations and Newspapers; Rules and Policies Concerning Multiple Ownership of Radio Broadcast Stations in Local Markets; Definition of Radio Markets; Definition of Radio Markets for Areas Not Located in an Arbitron Survey Area, MB Docket Nos. 02-277 and 03-130 and MM Docket Nos. 01-235, 01-3 17, and 00-244, Report and Order and Notice of Proposed Rulemaking (2003 Order), adopted June 2, 2003 and released July 2, 2003.

[6] *In the Matter of 2006 Quadrennial Regulatory Review — Review of the Commission's Broadcast Ownership Rules and Other Rules Adopted Pursuant to Section 202 of the Telecommunications Act of 1996; 2002 Biennial Regulatory Review — Review of the Commission's Broadcast Ownership Rules and Other Rules Adopted Pursuant to Section 202 of the Telecommunications Act of 1996; Cross-Ownership of Broadcast Stations and Newspapers; Rules and Policies Concerning Multiple Ownership of Radio Broadcast Stations in Local Markets; Definition of Radio Markets; Ways to Further Section 257 Mandate and to Build on Earlier Studies; Public Interest Obligations of TV Broadcast Licensees,* MB Docket Nos. 06-21, 02-277, and 04-228, and MM Docket Nos. 01-235, 01- 317, 00-244, and 99-360, Report and Order and Order on Reconsideration (2007 Order), adopted December 18, 2007, and released February 4, 2008, available at [http://hraunfoss.fcc.gov/ edocs_public/ attachmatch/ FCC-07-216A1.pdf], viewed on March 6, 2008. The specific language of the rule changes is presented in Appendix A of the 2007 Order.

[7] See "Statement of Commissioner Michael J. Copps, Dissenting," December 18, 2007, available at [http://hraunfoss.fcc.gov/edocs_public/attachmatch/ DOC-278932A3 .pdf], viewed on March 6, 2008, and "Statement of Commissioner Jonathan S. Adelstein, Dissenting," December 18, 2007, available at [http://hraunfoss.fcc.gov/edocs_public/ attachmatch/DOC-278932A4.pdf], viewed on March 6, 2008.

[8] 2007 Order, at paras. 13-79 and Appendix A, pp. 84-85..

[9] As explained in fn. 4 above, the Third Circuit, in its Prometheus decision, stated that it retained jurisdiction to review the FCC's action on remand, but when 15 parties filed appeals in a number of different circuit courts of appeal, the Ninth Circuit was chosen at random to hear the challenges.

[10] Ibid., at para. 77.

[11] Ibid., at Appendix A, p. 84, amending 47 C.F.R. 73.3555(d).

[12] Ibid., at Appendix A, pp. 84-85, amending 47 C.F.R. 73.3555(d)(3).

[13] Local markets are referred to as designated market areas or DMAs. DMAs are geographic designations developed by Nielsen Media Research. A DMA is made up of all the counties that get the preponderance of their broadcast programming from a given television market. The Nielsen DMAs are both complete (all counties in the United States are in a DMA) and exclusive (DMAs do not overlap). In the 1992 Cable Act, Congress amended the 1934 Communications Act to require, subject to certain exceptions, each cable system to carry the signals of all the local full power commercial television stations "within the same television market as the cable system," with that market determined by "commercial publications which delineate television markets based on viewing patterns." 47 U.S .C. § 534. The DMAs represent the only nationwide commercial mapping of television audience viewing patterns. Each county in the United States is assigned to a television market based on the viewing habits of the residents in the county.

[14] The rule defines major media voices as full-power commercial and noncommercial television stations and major newspapers, where the latter are those newspapers that are published at least four days a week within the DMA and have a circulation exceeding 5% of the households in the DMA. See 2007 Order, at Appendix A, p. 85, amending 47 C.F.R. 73.3555(d)(3)(ii).

[15] 2007 Order, at Appendix A, p. 85, amending 47 C.F.R. 73.3555(d)(4).

[16] Ibid., at Appendix A, p. 85, amending 47 C.F.R. 73.3555(d)(7).

[17] In order to qualify as failed, the newspaper or broadcast outlet has to have stopped circulation or have been dark for at least four months immediately prior to the filing of the assignment or transfer application, or must be involved in court-supervised involuntary bankruptcy or involuntary insolvency proceedings. To qualify as failing, the applicant must show that (a) the broadcast station has had an all-day audience share of 4% or lower; (b) the newspaper or broadcast station has had a negative cash flow for the previous three years; (c) the combination will produce public interest benefits; and (d) the in-market buyer is the only reasonably available candidate willing and able to acquire and operate the newspaper or station. See 2007 Order, at para. 65.

[18] 2007 Order, at Appendix A, p. 85, amending 47 C.F.R. 73.3555(d)(7)(ii).

[19] Ibid., at para. 67.

[20] Ibid., at Appendix A, p. 85, amending 47 C.F.R. 73.3555(d)(5) and (6).

[21] This factor, which has no numerical limits, is used to review all proposed newspaper- broadcast cross-ownership combinations and is distinct from one of the two criteria that would reverse a negative public interest

presumption — that the combination involve a broadcast station that has not been offering local news programming but post-combination would initiate seven hours of local newscasts.

[22] 2007 Order, at Appendix A, p. 85, amending 47 C.F.R. 73.3555(d)(6).

[23] Ibid., at paras. 68-75

[24] Ibid., at para. 68.

[25] Ibid., at para. 77.

[26] "Joint Statement by FCC Commissioners Michael J. Copps and Jonathan S. Adelstein on Release of Media Ownership Order," FCC New Release, February 4, 2008, available at [http://hraunfoss.fcc.gov/edocs_public/attachmatch/DOC-28000 1A1 .pdf], viewed on March 6, 2008.

[27] Since the new rule creates public interest presumptions based on numerical limits, but requires case-by-case public interest determinations that can supersede the numerical limits, it may well be that the courts will find that the burden on the FCC to justify the specific numerical limits is lower than the burden required to justify the rules in the 2003 Order.

[28] Ibid., at para. 56. The FCC also appears to rely on its finding that the top 20 markets, on average, have 15.5 major voices (independently owned television stations and major newspapers), 87.8 total voices (all independently owned television stations, radio stations, and major newspapers), and approximately 3.3 million television households, while markets 21 through 30, by comparison, have, on average, 9.5 major voices, 65.0 total voices, and fewer than 1.1 million television households. A comparison of these averages for the top 20 markets and the 21st through 30th markets, however, does not address whether the bright line cutoff between the 20th and 21st markets is justified.

[29] Ibid., at para. 57.

[30] Ibid., at para. 58.

[31] Ibid., at para. 60.

[32] Ibid., at para. 61.

[33] Ibid., at para. 61.

[34] Ibid., at para. 62.

[35] However, the local affiliates of those four networks are not always the top-four rated stations in a market. In particular, in several markets with large Hispanic populations, the local Univision affiliate is among the four highest rated stations.

[36] 2007 Order, at para. 67.

[37] Ibid., at para. 70.

[38] Ibid., at Appendix A, p. 85, amending 47 C.F.R. 73.3555(d)(5)(i).

[39] Ibid., at Appendix A, p. 85, amending 47 C.F.R. 73.3555(d)(5)(i).

[40] See, for example, *In the Matter of 2006 Quadrennial Regulatory Review — Review of the Commission's Broadcast Ownership Rules and Other Rules Adopted Pursuant to Section 202 of the Telecommunications Act of 1996; 2002 Biennial Regulatory Review; Cross- Ownership of Broadcast Stations and Newspapers; Rules and Policies Concerning Multiple Ownership of Radio Broadcast Stations in Local Markets; Definition of Radio Markets; Ways to Further Section 257 Mandate and to Build on Earlier Studies*, MB Docket Nos. 06- 121, 02-277, and 04-228 and MM Docket Nos. 01-235, 01-317, and 00-244, Further Comments of Consumers Union, Consumer Federation of America, and Free Press, October 22, 2007.

[41] 2007 Order, at paras. 43-44.

[42] According to a "Broadcast" note in Communications Daily, March 7, 2008, the FCC's General Counsel's office identified more than 10 parties that appealed the rule change within 10 days of its publication in the Federal Register. Among the parties opposing any loosening of the rule are Prometheus Radio Project, Free Press, and the United Church of Christ. Among the parties favoring further loosening of the rule are Fox, Tribune, Sinclair, Bonneville, the Scranton Times, Cox Enterprises, Media General, the National Association of Broadcasters, and the Newspaper Association of America.

[43] "Quarter of Senate Writes FCC Threatening to Revoke Media Rule," *BNA, Inc. Daily Report for Executives*, December 18, 2007, at p. A-12.

[44] For a detailed discussion of the process required for a joint resolution of disapproval, see CRS Report RL301 16, *Congressional Review of Agency Rulemaking: An Update and Assessment of the Congressional Review Act After a Decade*, by Morton Rosenberg.

[45] Anne Veigle, "Dorgan Resolution Would Bar Media Ownership Rules," *Communications Daily*, March 6, 2008, at p. 1.

[46] Cheryl Bolen, "Advisers Would Recommend Veto of Resolution Overturning Media Rule," *BNA Inc. Daily Report for Executives*, April 3, 2008, at p. A-8.

[47] Anne Veigle, "Bush Veto Promised if Senate Rejects Media Ownership Rule," *Communications Daily*, May 16, 2008.

[48] S. 2332 and H.R. 4835 also would require the FCC to initiate, conduct, and complete a separate rulemaking to promote the broadcast of local programming and content; require the FCC to establish an independent Panel on Women and Minority Ownership of Broadcast Media; and conduct a full and accurate census of the race and gender of broadcast owners.

[49] 47 C.F.R. 73.3555(c) as it existed prior to the FCC's June 2, 2003 Order. For this rule, media "voices" include independently owned and operating full-power broadcast television stations, broadcast radio stations, English-language newspapers (published at least four times a week), one cable system located in the market under scrutiny, plus any independently owned out-of-market broadcast radio stations with a minimum share as reported by Arbitron.

[50] 2007 Order, at para. 82.

[51] Ibid., at para. 84.

[52] Ibid., at paras. 83-84.

[53] Grade B is a measure of signal intensity associated with acceptable reception. The FCC's rules define this contour, often a circle drawn around the transmitter site of a television station, in such a way that 50 percent of the locations on that circle are statistically predicted to receive a signal of Grade B intensity at least 90 per cent of the time. Although a station's predicted signal strength increases as one gets closer to the transmitter, there will still be some locations within the predicted Grade B contour that do not receive a signal of Grade B intensity.

[54] 47 C.F.R. 73.3555(b); Local TV Ownership Report and Order, 14 FCC Rcd at 12907-08, para. 8.

[55] A "failed" station is one that has been dark for at least four months or is involved in court-supervised involuntary bankruptcy or involuntary insolvency proceedings. Under the standard for "failing" stations, a waiver is presumed to be in the public interest if the applicant satisfies each of the following criteria: (1) one of the merging stations has had all- day audience share of 4% or lower; (2) the financial condition of one of the merging stations is poor; (3) and the merger will produce public interest benefits. Under the standard for "unbuilt" stations, a waiver is presumed to be in the public interest if an applicant meets each of the following criteria: (1) the combination will result in the construction of an authorized but as yet unbuilt station; and (2) the permittee has made reasonable efforts to construct, and has been unable to do so. (47 C.F.R. 73.3555, Note 7 (1) and Local Television Ownership Report, 14 FCC Rcd at 12941, para. 86.

[56] *Local TV Ownership Report and Order,* 14 FCC Rcd at 12938-41, paras. 77, 81, 86.

[57] 2007 Order, at para. 87.

[58] Ibid., at para. 101.

[59] Ibid., at para. 103.

[60] 2007 Order, at paras. 96 and 105.

[61] *Prometheus,* 373 F.3d at 420-421.

[62] Section 202(b) also provides that the commission may permit a party to exceed these limits "if the Commission determines that [it] will result in an increase in the number of radio broadcast stations in operation." 1996 Act, § 202(b)(2), 110 Stat. at 10-11.

[63] 2003 Order, at para. 239.

[64] Ibid., at para. 239.

[65] Ibid., at para. 239.

[66] 2007 Order, at paras. 110, 116, 117, and 123.

[67] Ibid., at para. 118.

[68] Ibid., at para. 124.

[69] Ibid., at para. 128.

[70] Ibid., at para. 134.

[71] These requirements all are in Section 629 of the FY2004 Consolidated Appropriations Act (P.L. 108-109, 118 Stat. 3 et seq.). The relevant FCC rule is 47 C.F.R. 73.3555(d)(1).

[72] The Third Circuit concluded that challenges to the FCC's decision to retain the 50% UHF "discount" were moot "because reducing or eliminating the discount for UHF station audiences would effectively raise the audience reach limit ... [which] would undermine Congress's specification of a precise 39% cap." (Prometheus, 373 F.3d at 396). The relevant FCC rule is 47 C.F.R. 73.3555(d)(2)(i).

[73] 2007 Order, at para. 143.

[74] Ibid., at para. 144.

[75] 47 C.F.R. 73.658(g).

[76] See 2003 Order, at para. 592, and 2007 Order, at para. 139.

[77] *Prometheus*, 373 F.3d at 421, footnote 59.

[78] *In the Matter of Promoting Diversification of Ownership in the Broadcasting Services; 2006 Quadrennial Regulatory Review — Review of the Commission's Broadcast Ownership Rules and Other Rules Adopted Pursuant to Section 202 of the Telecommunications Act of 1996; 2002 Biennial Regulatory Review — Review of the Commission's Broadcast Ownership Rules and Other Rules Adopted Pursuant to Section 202 of the Telecommunications Act of 1996; Cross-Ownership of Broadcast Stations an Newspapers; Rules and Policies Concerning Multiple Ownership of Radio Broadcast Stations in Local Markets*; Definition of Radio Markets; Ways to Further Section 257 Mandate and to Build on Earlier Studies, MB Docket Nos. 07-294, 06-12 1, 02-277, and 04-228 and MM Docket Nos. 01-235, 01-3 17, and 00-244, Report and Order and Third Further Notice of

Proposed Rule Making, adopted on December 18, 2007 and released on March 5, 2008, available at [http://hraunfoss.fcc.gov/edocs_public/ attachmatch/FCC-07-2 17A1 .pdf], viewed on March 5, 2008.

[79] Commissioners Copps and Adelstein dissented in part from the order because they were concerned that people of color and women would not benefit appreciably from, and might be harmed by, these programs if eligibility is not specifically targeted to socially and economically disadvantaged businesses. See "Statement of Commissioner Michael J. Copps, Concur in Part, Dissent in Part," December 18, 2007, available at [http://hraunfoss.fcc.gov/edocs_public/attachmatch/DOC-279035A3 .pdf], viewed on March 6, 2008, and "Statement of Commissioner Jonathan S. Adelstein, Concur in Part, Dissent in Part," December 18, 2007, available at [http://hraunfoss.fcc.gov/edocs_public/ attachmatch/DOC-279035A4.pdf], viewed on March 6, 2008.

[80] 280 F.3d 1048.

[81] 293 F.3d 539.

[82] 293 F.3d 540.

[83] *Prometheus*, 373 F.3d at 394 (emphasis in original).

[84] 2003 Order at paras. 80-85. In the section on Policy Goals, there are four subsections — Diversity, Competition, Localism, and Regulatory Certainty.

[85] Ibid., at para. 83, fn. Omitted.

[86] Ibid., at para. 453, fn. 980.

[87] *Prometheus*, 373 F.3d at 431.

[88] 2007 Order, at para. 46.

[89] Ibid., at para. 52.

[90] See, for example, 2007 Order, at para. 113.

[91] Ibid., at para. 77.

[92] *In the Matter of Shareholders of Tribune Company, Transferors and Sam Zell, et al., Transferees, for Consent to the Transfer of Control of the Tribune Company and Applications for the Renewal of License of KTLA(TV), Los Angeles, California, et al.,* MB Docket No. 07-119 and File Nos. BRCT-200608 1 1ASH, et al., Memorandum Opinion and Order, adopted and released November 30, 2007. The Memorandum Opinion and Order and the statements of four commissioners, including the two dissenting commissioners, is available at [http://hraunfoss.fcc.gov/ edocs_public/attachmatch/FCC-07-21 1A1 .pdf], viewed on March 6, 2008.

[93] See, for example, "Tribune appeals FCC ruling," *Hollywood Reporter*, December 7, 2007.

[94] See fn. 90 above.

In: Media Ownership
Editor: Harold F. Velliotis, pp. 97-110
ISBN 978-1-60692-365-8

Chapter 3

TELECOMMUNICATIONS: PRELIMINARY INFORMATION ON MEDIA OWNERSHIP*

United States Government Accountability Office

The Honorable Edward J. Markey
Chairman
Subcommittee on Telecommunications and the Internet Committee on Energy and Commerce
House of Representatives

Subject: *Telecommunications: Preliminary Information on Media Ownership* Dear Mr. Chairman:

The media play an important role in educating and entertaining the public and fostering an informed citizenry; thus the ownership of media outlets has been a longstanding concern of the Congress. The Federal Communications Commission (FCC) regulates many aspects of the media industry, including radio and television stations and cable and satellite service. In the Telecommunications Act of 1996 (1996 Act), the Congress required that FCC periodically review its media ownership rules. In 2003, FCC released an order that altered its existing media ownership rules. This order generated significant public debate, and more than 500,000 comments were filed with FCC. The U.S. Court of Appeals for the Third

* Excerpted fro GAO Report 08-330R, dated December 14, 2007.

Circuit affirmed some of FCC's rule changes while remanding others for further justification or modification; [1] most of the rule changes have not gone into effect. In response to the court's decision and the congressional mandate for periodic review of its rules, FCC has another proceeding underway to assess its media ownership rules. This proceeding has attracted significant attention from both the public and the Congress, and has raised concerns about the level of consolidation in the media industry.

While today's media environment provides the public with numerous programming choices from across the country, media outlets in local markets remain a concern for policymakers. With cable and satellite service, the public can receive programming from nationwide outlets, such as CNN and FOX News, and television stations in adjacent markets. However, media outlets located in a market are more likely to provide local news, public affairs, and political programming addressing the needs of residents in that market, such as coverage of local political campaigns, compared to nationwide and adjacent-market outlets. Reflecting the importance of local media outlets, localism is one of FCC's three policy goals for media ownership.

You asked us to examine the current status of media ownership. In this report, we provide preliminary information on (1) the presence and ownership of various media outlets, (2) the level of minority- and women-owned broadcast outlets, and (3) stakeholders' opinions on modifying certain media ownership laws and regulations. We plan to issue a final report on this work in several months.

To respond to the objectives of this report, we interviewed officials from FCC, the National Telecommunications and Information Administration (NTIA) of the Department of Commerce, and trade associations. Additionally, we conducted structured interviews with 102 industry officials and experts, selected based on industry sector (such as television and radio stations, broadcast networks, newspapers, and cable and satellite companies), geographic service territory, size of the media outlet, and professional publications (for experts). To assess the presence and ownership of media outlets, we conducted case studies in Nielsen Designated Market Areas (DMA) [2]. To select the case study markets, we used a stratified random sample methodology: we (1) randomly selected four case study markets from each of three market strata (large, medium, and small), (2) selected the three largest markets as a separate stratum, and (3) judgmentally selected one market from the medium-size category to test our data collection and structured interview methodology. The case study markets that we analyzed include approximately 20 percent of all television households in the United States. In each case study market, we identified the number of television and radio stations, newspapers (daily and weekly), and cable and satellite companies present in the central city of the DMA.

We also identified the number of owners of these media outlets.

We conducted our review from February 2007 through December 2007 in accordance with generally accepted government auditing standards.

RESULTS IN BRIEF

The numbers of media outlets and owners of media outlets generally increase with the size of the market, although operating agreements may reduce the effective number of independent outlets. Markets with large populations have more television and radio stations and newspapers than less-populated markets. For example, in New York City, the nation's largest market, we identified 21 television stations and 73 radio stations. In contrast, we found 2 television stations and radio stations in Harrisonburg, Virginia, the smallest market in our review. In more diverse markets, we also observed more radio and television stations and newspapers operating in languages other than English, which contributed to a greater number of outlets. While we focused on media outlets located in specific markets, residents, in some instances, may be able to receive television and radio signals from stations located in adjacent markets. Some companies participate in agreements to share content or agreements that allow one company to produce programming or sell advertising through two outlets, among other agreements. In our review, these agreements were prevalent in a variety of markets but not in the top three markets, suggesting that market size may influence the benefits that companies realize through such agreements. To some degree, these agreements may suggest that the number of independently owned media outlets in a market might not always be a good indicator of how many independently produced local news or other programs are available in a market.

Ownership of broadcast outlets by minorities and women appears limited, but comprehensive data are lacking. FCC collects data on the gender, race, and ethnicity of radio and television station owners biennially through its Ownership Report for Commercial Broadcast Stations, or Form 323. However, we found that these data suffer from three weaknesses: (1) exemptions from filing for certain types of broadcast stations, such as noncommercial stations; (2) inadequate data quality procedures; and (3) problems with data storage and retrieval. While reliable government data on the ownership by minorities and women are lacking, available evidence from FCC and nongovernmental reports suggests that ownership of broadcast outlets by these groups is limited. For example, reports by

Free Press, a nongovernmental organization, found that women and minorities own about 5 percent and 3 percent of full-power televisions stations, respectively, and about 6 percent and 8 percent of full-power radio stations, respectively.

Stakeholders expressed varied opinions about the media ownership rules under review by FCC. Among the stakeholders we interviewed, there was little consensus on modifications to existing laws and regulations related to media ownership. However, stakeholders representing business interests were more likely to support deregulatory positions while nonbusiness stakeholders were more likely to support enhancing or leaving existing rules in place. Moreover, both business and nonbusiness stakeholders who expressed an opinion on a previously repealed tax certificate program supported either reinstating or expanding the program to encourage the sale of broadcast outlets to minorities.

BACKGROUND

Various laws and regulations constrain the ownership of television and radio stations. Five restrictions on the ownership of television and radio stations follow:

- *National television ownership cap.* A single entity can own any number of television stations nationwide as long as the stations collectively reach no more than 39 percent of national television households. For purposes of calculating the 39 percent limit, ultra-high frequency (UHF) television stations are attributed with 50 percent of the television households in their market.
- *Local television ownership limit.* A single entity can own two television stations in the same DMA if (1) the "Grade B" contours [3] of the stations do not overlap or (2) at least one of the stations is not ranked among the top four stations in terms of audience share and at least eight independently owned and operating full-power commercial and noncommercial television stations would remain in the DMA. In general, no entity can own more than two television stations whose Grade B contours overlap regardless of whether (1) the stations are not among the top four stations in terms of audience share and (2) at least eight independently owned and operating full-power commercial and noncommercial stations would remain in the DMA.
- *Local radio ownership limit.* A single entity can own up to 5 commercial radio stations, not more than 3 of which are in the same service (that is,

AM or FM), in a market with 14 or fewer radio stations; up to 6 commercial radio stations, not more than 4 of which are in the same service, in a market with 15 to 29 radio stations; up to 7 commercial radio stations, not more than 4 of which are in the same service, in a market with 30 to 44 radio stations; and up to 8 commercial radio stations, not more than 5 of which are in the same service, in a market with 45 or more radio stations; except that an entity can not own, operate, or control more than 50 percent of the stations in a market [4].

- *Newspaper-broadcast cross-ownership ban.* A single entity cannot have common ownership of a full-service television or radio station and a daily newspaper [5] if the television station's "Grade A" contour or the radio station's principal community service area completely encompass the newspaper's city of publication [6].
- *Television-radio cross-ownership limit.* A single entity can own up to 2 television stations (if permitted under the Local Television Multiple Ownership Cap) and up to 6 radio stations (if permitted under the Local Radio Multiple Ownership Cap) or 1 television station and 7 radio stations in a market with at least 20 independently owned media voices remaining post merger; up to 2 television stations and up to 4 radio stations in a market with at least 10 independently owned media voices remaining post merger; and 1 television station and 1 radio station regardless of the number of independently owned media voices [7].

In the 1996 Act, the Congress required FCC to conduct a biennial review of its media ownership rules to determine "whether any such rules are necessary in the public interest as the result of competition" and to "repeal or modify any regulation it determines to be no longer in the public interest." [8]. In its 2002 biennial review, FCC adopted several important changes to its media ownership regulations. FCC increased the caps on ownership of local television stations, increased the nationwide television ownership cap, eliminated the prohibition on joint ownership of a broadcast outlet and a newspaper in some instances, and raised the caps on joint ownership of television and radio stations in local markets. In 2004, the U.S. Court of Appeals for the Third Circuit affirmed some of FCC's rule changes while remanding others for further justification or modification; most of the rule changes have not gone into effect. In 2006, FCC released a Further Notice of Proposed Rule Making concerning its media ownership rules [9]. FCC initiated the rule making to address the issues posed by the Court of Appeals as well as to fulfill the congressional mandate for periodic review of its media ownership rules [10].

Since the 1970s, the number of media outlets has increased dramatically, with large increases in the number of television and radio stations. In the case of television, the number of full-power television stations increased from 875 in 1970 to 1,754 in 2006; this increase occurred in both commercial and noncommercial educational television stations [11]. Moreover, the number of broadcast networks that supply programming to stations across the country increased from three major networks (ABC, CBS, and NBC) to four major networks (ABC, CBS, FOX, and NBC) and several smaller networks, such as The CW Television Network, MY Network TV, and ION Television Network. In the case of radio, the number of full-power radio stations more than doubled, from 6,751 stations in 1970 to 13,793 stations in 2006, with increases in AM, FM, and FM educational stations [12]. Daily newspapers illustrate a different trend—decreasing from 1,763 in 1970 to 1,447 in 2006. While the number of morning newspapers increased from 334 in 1970 to 833 in 2006, the number of evening newspapers decreased by more than half, from 1,429 to 614. Table 1 illustrates the trends in television and radio stations and newspapers.

While the number of media outlets has increased, the ownership of outlets also has evolved. Beginning in the late 1980s, the broadcast networks increasingly have become affiliated with companies that provide program production services, as happened when The Walt Disney Company acquired ABC. Each of the four major broadcast networks also owns television stations that reach more than 20 percent of the nation's television households. Following the passage of the 1996 Act, several companies acquired a large number of radio stations. Clear Channel owns over 1,000 radio stations throughout the United States, and Cumulus Broadcasting and Citadel Communications each own over 200 stations.

Table 1. Number of Full-Power Television and Radio Stations and Daily Newspapers

Media category	Number of outlets by year		
	1970	1990	2006
Television station	875	1,465	1,754
Radio station	6,751	10,770	13,793
Daily newspaper	1,763	1,643	1,447
Morning	334	559	833
Evening	1,429	1,084	614

Source: GAO analysis of data from FCC and the Newspaper Association of America.

Finally, four companies—Comcast, DirecTV, Time Warner, and EchoStar—provide service to nearly two-thirds of subscribers to cable television or direct broadcast satellite service; additionally, many nonbroadcast networks, such as CNN and ESPN, are owned by cable companies or broadcast networks [13].

In recent years, some companies have taken steps to sell assets. In 2005, Viacom split into two separate companies: Viacom and CBS Corporation [14]. In 2006, The McClatchy Company acquired Knight Ridder and subsequently sold 12 former Knight Ridder newspapers. Also in 2006, Clear Channel announced plans to sell 448 radio stations, all in markets outside the top 100, and its entire television station group [15]. More recently, The New York Times Company sold its television stations. Alternatively, the two satellite radio companies—Sirius and XM—have proposed a merger that, if approved, would leave one company providing satellite radio service.

Numbers of Media Outlets and Owners Generally Increase with Market Size, Although Operating Agreements May Reduce the Effective Number of Independent Outlets

Markets with large populations have more television, radio, and newspaper outlets than less populated markets. In the top three markets—New York, Los Angeles, and Chicago—the combination of large populations and relatively high disposable income helps produce substantial advertising revenues for the media outlets in these markets. Hence, these markets have more television and radio stations and more newspapers than other markets. Alternatively, the small markets we analyzed—such as Jackson, Tennessee, and Harrisonburg, Virginia—are characterized by significantly fewer media outlets than larger markets. In more diverse markets, we also observed more radio and television stations and newspapers operating in languages other than English, which contributed to a greater number of outlets. For example, the Miami/Fort Lauderdale, Florida, market has more television stations than the other large, case study markets we studied because of the large number of Spanish language outlets. In addition, the Tucson, Arizona, market, which has a relatively large Hispanic population, has more television and radio stations than other similarly sized case study markets due to the presence of Spanish language television and radio stations. Table 2 illustrates the number of media outlets and owners in our case study markets [16]. While we focused on media outlets located in specific markets, residents may, in some instances, be able to receive television and radio signals from stations located in adjacent markets.

Table 2. Number of Media Outlets and Owners in Case Study Markets

Case study market	Television stations		Radio stations		Daily newspapers	
Name (DMA rank)	Outlets	Owners	Outlets	Owners	Outlets	Owners
New York, New York (1)	21	15	73	44	5	5
Los Angeles, California (2)	24	19	69	34	2	2
Chicago, Illinois (3)		13	65	38	3	3
Miami, Florida ()		13	47	24	3	2
Charlotte, North Carolina (26)	12	9	37	17	1	1
Nashville, Tennessee (30)	12	11	52	35	2	2
Scranton, Pennsylvania (53)	8	7	24	14	1	1
Tucson, Arizona (70)	11	8	38	17	2	2
Springfield, Missouri (76)	6	6	26	11	2	2
Chattanooga, Tennessee (86)	8	8	32	20	1	1
Cedar Rapids, Iowa (89)	9	8	25	11	1	1
Florence, South Carolina (105)	6	5	13	6	1	1
Terre Haute, Indiana (151)	5	5	18	11	1	1
Sherman, Texas (1)	2	2	23	13	1	1
Jackson, Tennessee (174)	3	3	21	14	1	1
Harrisonburg, Virginia (181)	2	2		7	1	1

Source: GAO analysis of FCC data, Warren Online Cable and Television Factbook, and Bowker's News Media Directory.

Some media companies participate in operating agreements that involve a partnership between two or more outlets. For example, some companies participate in agreements wherein one company produces content or sells advertising through its own outlets and another company's outlets. FCC's attribution rules—which seek to identify those interests in or relationships to licensees that have a realistic potential to affect the programming decisions of licensees or other core operating functions— apply to several types of operating agreements [17].

In our case study markets, we found these agreements in a variety of markets but not in the top 3 markets, suggesting that market size may influence the benefits that companies realize through such agreements. We found television stations participating in operating agreements in five markets—Nashville, Tennessee; Wilkes Barre/Scranton, Pennsylvania; Springfield, Missouri; Myrtle Beach/Florence, South Carolina; and Terre Haute, Indiana. We also found operating agreements between radio stations in Harrisonburg, Virginia, and Nashville, Tennessee; and in Tucson, Arizona, the two competing daily newspapers participate in a joint operating agreement [18]. To some extent, these agreements may reduce the number of independent outlets. For example, in

Wilkes Barre/Scranton, we identified eight television stations. However, one owner of two stations participated in an agreement with a third station and the remaining four television stations participated in two separate agreements—each agreement covering two stations. Thus, while there are eight television stations and seven owners in Wilkes Barre/Scranton, there are three loose commercial groupings in the market. This example suggests that the number of independently owned media outlets in a given market is not always a good indicator of how many independently produced local news or other programs are available in a market.

Ownership of Broadcast Outlets by Women and Minorities Appears Limited, but Comprehensive Data Are Lacking

In 1998, FCC issued rules to collect data on the gender, race, and ethnicity of holders of broadcast licenses. FCC decided to collect these data via its Ownership Report for Commercial Broadcast Stations, or Form 323. FCC noted that it was appropriate to develop "precise information on minority and female ownership of mass media facilities" and "annual information on the state and progress of minority and female ownership," thereby positioning "both Congress and the Commission to assess the need for, and success of, programs to foster opportunities for minorities and females to own broadcast facilities."[19] FCC began collecting these data in 1999 and the Form 323 is the only mechanism through which FCC collects information on the gender, race, and ethnicity of broadcast owners; FCC requires biennial filing of the Form 323.

As FCC's only information source on owners' gender, race, and ethnicity, the Form 323 data potentially could be used to determine and periodically report on the level of women and minority broadcast ownership. However, we identified several weaknesses that limit the usefulness of the Form 323 data [20]

- *Filing exemptions.* Sole proprietors, partnerships, and noncommercial stations are not required to file the Form 323 [21]. Since data from the Form 323 do not include stations owned by sole proprietors, partnerships, or noncommercial stations, it is not possible to use the Form 323 data to identify either the full universe of broadcast stations owned by women and minorities or the number of women and minority owners. FCC also does not require the filing of the Form 323 for low-power stations.

- *Data quality procedures.* According to FCC officials, FCC does not verify or periodically review the gender, race, and ethnicity data submitted via the Form 323. According to these officials, a staff person from FCC's Video Division reviews submitted Form 323s, and this staff person focuses on ensuring compliance with the commission's multiple ownership and citizen ownership rules. These officials told us that station owners were responsible for determining the accuracy of their Form 323 submissions.
- *Data storage and retrieval.* Companies must file the Form 323 electronically. However, FCC allows owners to provide attachments with their electronic filing of the Form 323. These attachments may include the gender, race, and ethnicity data. Since these data are not entered into the database, the data are unavailable for electronic query.

While there are no reliable government data on ownership by women and minorities, ownership of broadcast outlets by these groups appears limited. According to the industry stakeholders and experts we interviewed, the level is limited, and recent studies generally support this conclusion. In a 2006 report, Free Press found that for full-power television stations, women and minority ownership was about 5 percent and 3 percent, respectively. Specifically, the report noted that women owned a majority stake in 67 of 1,349 full power commercial television stations and minorities owned 44 stations, 8 of which were owned by 1 company. In another report, Free Press estimated that women owned approximately 629 of 10,506 (or 6 percent) of full- power radio stations and minorities owned 812 stations (or 8 percent) of full-power radio stations. Additionally, three reports commissioned by FCC as part of its media ownership proceeding found relatively limited levels of ownership of television and radio stations by women and minorities.

Stakeholders' Opinions Varied on Modifications to Media Ownership Rules, but Business Stakeholders Were More Likely to Favor Deregulation

The stakeholders we interviewed seldom agreed on proposed modifications to media ownership rules. However, business stakeholders expressing opinions on these rules were more likely to report that the rules should be relaxed or repealed. In contrast, nonbusiness stakeholders who expressed opinions on the rules were more likely to report that the rules should be left in place or strengthened. Both business and nonbusiness stakeholders who expressed an opinion on a previously repealed tax certificate program supported either reinstating or expanding the program to encourage the sale of broadcast outlets to minorities.

- *National television ownership cap.* The majority (65 of 102) of stakeholders expressed no opinion on this issue. Of the 37 who did express an opinion, 22 said the cap should be left as is or lowered, further restricting ownership, while 15 favored raising or repealing the cap. But these results differed for nonbusiness and business stakeholders. Whereas 11 of 15 nonbusiness stakeholders stated that the cap should be left as is or lowered, further restricting ownership, 11 of 22 business stakeholders indicated that the cap should raised or repealed.
- *Local television and radio ownership limits.* Stakeholders were fairly evenly divided on whether FCC should alter rules limiting the number of television and radio stations a single entity can own in a local market. Of the 50 stakeholders expressing an opinion on the matter, 27 said the rule should be repealed and 23 said the rule should either be left as is or strengthened. However, opinions within stakeholder segments were more consistent. Fourteen of 19 nonbusiness stakeholders were in favor of strengthening or leaving the rules in place, while 22 of 31 business stakeholders were in favor of repealing the regulation.
- *Newspaper-broadcast cross-ownership ban.* Overall, stakeholders were fairly evenly divided on whether FCC should modify its current rule prohibiting cross- ownership of newspapers and television or radio stations in the same local area. Of the 50 stakeholders expressing an opinion on the matter, 27 reported that the rule should be repealed and 23 said the rule should either be left as is or strengthened. However, among business and nonbusiness stakeholders interviewed, there were clear differences in opinion on this issue. Fourteen of 20 nonbusiness stakeholders were in favor of strengthening or leaving the rule in place. In contrast, 21 of 30 business stakeholders were in favor of repealing the regulation. For example, 13 of 14 stakeholders from multisector media companies stated the rule should be repealed.
- *Reinstitution of minority tax certificate program.* Prior to its repeal by the Congress in 1995, the minority tax certificate program provided for the seller of a broadcast station to defer capital gains taxes on the sale if the station was sold to a minority-owned company. Of the 102 stakeholders interviewed, most (72) expressed no opinion as to whether the minority

tax certificate program should be reinstated. However, among the 30 stakeholders who mentioned this issue, there was broad consensus in favor of reinstating some version of this program. Twenty-eight of these 30 stakeholders indicated that either the program should be reintroduced without changes or expanded, and 2 said the program was not needed and should not be reinstated.

AGENCY COMMENTS

We provided a draft of this report to FCC for its review and comment. FCC provided technical comments that we incorporated where appropriate. In addition, FCC noted that it has several items under consideration that could impact media ownership.

As agreed with your office, unless you publicly announce the contents of this report earlier, we plan no further distribution until 30 days from the report date. At that time, we will send copies of this report to the Chairman of the Federal Communications Commission and interested congressional committees. We will also make copies available to others upon request. In addition, the report will be available at no charge on the GAO Web site at http://www.gao.gov.

If you have any questions about this report, please contact me at (202) 512-2834 or heckerj@gao.gov. Individuals making key contributions to this report include Michael Clements (Assistant Director), Carl Barden, Matt Barranca, Steve Brown, Ted Burik, Elizabeth Eisenstadt, Brandon Haller, Madhav Panwar, Friendly VangJohnson, and Mindi Weisenbloom.

JayEtta Z. Hecker
Director, Physical Infrastructure Issues

REFERENCES

[1] Prometheus Radio Project v. FCC, 373 F.3d 372 (3rd Cir. 2004), cert. denied, 545 U.S. 1123 (2005).

[2] According to Nielsen, a DMA consists of all counties whose largest viewing share is given to stations of the same market area. There are 210

nonoverlapping DMAs that cover the entire continental United States, Hawaii, and parts of Alaska.

[3] "Grade B" is an FCC-defined measure of signal strength pertaining to the availability of an over-the-air signal with a rooftop antenna.

[4] There is no limit on the number of AM or FM radio stations that a single entity can own nationwide.

[5] For purposes of this rule, a daily newspaper is defined as one published 4 or more days per week in English and circulated generally in the community of publication; the definition includes non-English newspapers if published in the primary language of the market.

[6] Newspaper-broadcast combinations that predate imposition of this ban are permitted. Companies also may seek a waiver from FCC to permit a newspaper-broadcast combination.

[7] For purposes of this rule, media voices include independently owned and operating full-power television stations, radio stations, daily newspapers with a circulation that exceeds 5 percent of the households in the DMA, one cable system if that system is generally available to households in the DMA, and independently owned out-of-market radio stations with a minimum share as reported by Arbitron.

[8] See Telecommunications Act of 1996, Pub. L. No. 104-104, 110 Stat. 56, Section 202(h).

[9] *2006 Quadrennial Regulatory Review—Review of the Commission's Broadcast Ownership Rules and Other Rules Adopted Pursuant to Section 202 of the Telecommunications Act of 1996,* Further Notice of Proposed Rulemaking, 21 FCC Rcd. 8834 (2006).

[10] The Congress now requires FCC to review its broadcast media ownership rules every 4 years.

[11] In addition to full-power television stations, there were approximately 568 Class A and 2,227 low- power television stations in 2006.

[12] In addition to full-power radio stations, there were approximately 770 low-power FM stations in 2006.

[13] For example, among the nonbroadcast networks with the most subscribers, CNN and TNT are affiliated with Time Warner, ESPN is affiliated with Disney, USA Network is affiliated with NBC- Universal, and Discovery Channel is affiliated with Cox.

[14] These two separate companies are controlled by National Amusements, Inc.

[15] On November 13, 2007, FCC granted, subject to conditions, Clear Channel's application to assign its television stations to Newport Television

LLC, which is wholly owned by affiliates of Providence Equity Partners, Inc.

[16] The other large media markets in our case study analysis are Charlotte, North Carolina; Nashville, Tennessee; and Wilkes Barre/Scranton, Pennsylvania

[17] We did not review whether the agreements fell within the requirements of the attribution rules.

[18] The Newspaper Preservation Act of 1970 allows various operating agreements in order "to preserve separate and independent editorial voices."

[19] *1998 Biennial Regulatory Review—Streamlining of Mass Media Applications, Rules, and Processes; Policies and Rules Regarding Minority and Female Ownership of Mass Media Facilities;* Report and Order, 13 FCC Rcd. 23056, 23096-23097 (1998).

[20] For its media ownership proceeding, FCC commissioned three studies assessing the status of women and minority broadcast ownership. Each of the three studies explored the adequacy of FCC's Form 323 data records and found the aggregate data to be unreliable.

[21] Noncommercial stations are required to file a Form 323-E. However, the Form 323-E does not collect data on gender, race, or ethnicity.

INDEX

A

B

E

F

G

H

I

Q

R

S